ENEMY OFFSHORE!

Japan's Secret War on North America's West Coast

BRENDAN COYLE

AND

MELANIE ARNIS

HERITAGE

VICTORIA · VANCOUVER · CALGARY

Heritage House Publishing Company Ltd.
heritagehouse.ca

Library and Archives Canada Cataloguing in Publication
Coyle, Brendan, 1957-, author
    Enemy offshore! : Japan's secret war on North America's West Coast / Brendan Coyle and Melanie Arnis.

(Amazing stories)
Issued in print and electronic formats.
ISBN 978-1-927527-53-5 (pbk.)—ISBN 978-1-927527-54-2 (epub)—ISBN 978-1-927527-55-9 (pdf)

1. World War, 1939-1945—Northwest Coast of North America. 2. World War, 1939-1945—Aerial operations, Japanese. 3. World War, 1939-1945—Naval operations—Submarine. 4. World War, 1939-1945—Naval operations, Japanese. 5. Northwest Coast of North America—History. I. Arnis, Melanie, author II. Title. III. Series: Amazing stories (Victoria, B.C.)

D767.2.C688 2013   940.54'28   C2013-903387-4   C2013-903388-2

Series editor: Lesley Reynolds
Proofreader: Liesbeth Leatherbarrow

Cover photo: Point Atkinson lighthouse. Major Matthews Collection, City of Vancouver Archives AM54-S4-: Out N140.

 **MIX**
Paper from
responsible sources
FSC® C016245

The interior of this book was produced on 30% post-consumer recycled paper, processed chlorine free and printed with vegetable-based inks.

Heritage House acknowledges the financial support for its publishing program from the Government of Canada through the Canada Book Fund (CBF), Canada Council for the Arts and the province of British Columbia through the British Columbia Arts Council and the Book Publishing Tax Credit.

 Canadian Patrimoine
Heritage canadien   Canada Council Conseil des Arts
for the Arts du Canada   BRITISH COLUMBIA
ARTS COUNCIL

17 16 15 14 13 1 2 3 4 5
Printed in Canada

Contents

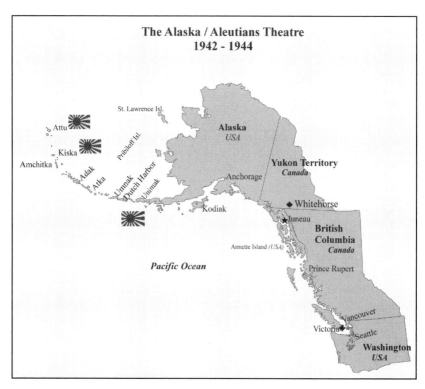

The Alaska / Aleutians Theatre
1942 - 1944

St. Lawrence Isl.

Alaska
USA

Yukon Territory
Canada

Attu

Kiska

Amchitka

Pribilof Isl.

Adak

Atka

Anchorage

Unmak
Dutch Harbor
Unimak

Kodiak

Whitehorse

Juneau

British
Columbia
Canada

Annette Island *(USA)*

Prince Rupert

Pacific Ocean

Vancouver

Victoria

Seattle

Washington
USA

This map shows the extent of the Japanese advance into Alaska. Japanese planes launched from the carriers *Ryujo* and *Junyo* bombed Dutch Harbor in two attacks on June 3 and 4, 1942, and seized the islands of Attu and Kiska. BRENDAN COYLE

Prologue

ON THE MORNING OF DECEMBER 7, 1941, *a lone steamer out of Seattle made her slow way across the Pacific, heading south toward Hawaii. Loaded on* Cynthia Olson's *open decks was dressed lumber, cut and milled in Tacoma, Washington, and bound for military construction in Honolulu. As the ship's old steam engines cranked toward those volcanic islands, still some thousand miles away, her 31 crewmen were unaware that Japanese Imperial Navy planes were barrelling toward Pearl Harbor in Hawaii.*

But Cynthia Olson *and her crew faced a much more immediate threat. As she continued on her way, her skipper, Berthel Carlsen, was oblivious of the Japanese submarine that had the freighter in its sights. Aboard the submarine,*

Captain Minoru Yakota, commander of I-26, glanced at his wristwatch and made note of the time. Within minutes, Admiral Yamamoto's forces would strike the United States Pacific Fleet at Pearl Harbor and the two nations would be at war. Then, and only then, could I-26 commence warfare against American ships. A premature attack might alert the US forces of Japan's intentions before the American fleet at Pearl Harbor was bombed. Until that time, Yakota could only shadow the unsuspecting Cynthia Olson *and her crew.*

Yakota glanced at his watch again. The first wave of attack planes should now be closing on Pearl Harbor's battleship row. Yakota ticked off another five minutes and then gave the order to surface. The first officer relayed the order, initiating a sequence that blasted compressed air into the ballast tanks, purging the water that held the submarine down and bringing I-26 to the surface in a froth of air and water.

On deck, the gun crew loaded one shell into the 140-millimetre (5.5-inch) deck cannon and fired it across Cynthia Olson's *bow. Unheeding or unaware of the shot across the bow, the crew did not respond. Taken aback, Yakota ordered a second warning shot. This time* Cynthia Olson's *crew noticed and heaved to. As the two vessels bobbed in the waves, Yakota allowed the freighter's crew to abandon ship in two lifeboats. Not fearing any immediate enemy response, he told his crew to open fire with the deck gun and, circling the ship, put his crew members through various attack angles. This manoeuvre went on for several hours, but the stubborn* Cynthia Olson, *held afloat by its cargo of lumber, refused to sink. Yakota ordered a torpedo fired, but it went wildly off course. Believing American planes might appear at any moment, he then submerged his boat to consider the situation.*

While the Cynthia Olson's *crew were abandoning ship, the freighter's wireless operator had sent off two SOS messages, alerting the liner* Lurline, *600 kilometres to the south, that they were under attack by submarine.* Lurline *relayed the SOS to San Francisco, but the message was met with confusion as no word had yet come over the airwaves about an enemy attack on Hawaii.*

After 35 minutes, Yakota ordered the sub to surface again to fire more rounds into the ship. He remained there for seven hours, surprised that he had not spotted a single American aircraft. With his quarry aflame and settling to port, Yakota was satisfied the ship was now a total loss. With a low grind of diesel engines, I-26 proceeded to the northeast on a course that would bring it to the waters off Washington State and British Columbia. Cynthia Olson's *crew were left drifting in the Pacific.*

Introduction

IN THE DECADES FOLLOWING THE Second World War, rumours from the war years that seemed to be based more on imagination than fact swirled around the West Coast—a Japanese submarine had been sunk off Victoria after firing on the city, a Japanese Zero had flown over downtown Portland, Oregon, and the Japanese had actually bombed Anchorage, Alaska.

Some of those rumours had a bit of truth in them. While Japanese submarines didn't shell Victoria, they did bombard the West Coast—and more than once. An enemy aircraft did fly over Oregon and bombed it in an almost unnoticed attack. And while the Zeros didn't make it as far as Anchorage, they did attack Dutch Harbor. So while the

Pacific war seemed well removed from the solitude of the West Coast, Japan brought it to North American shores and grabbed a toehold there. The enemy actions offshore served to create a climate of fear and suspicion, which certainly had lasting consequences for West Coast residents of Japanese ancestry.

In 1934, Japan had renounced the Washington Naval Treaty that had limited her navy strength; the invasion of China followed in 1937. Being an island nation, the country had limited room for growth. Japan's rulers looked longingly at the vast colonial empires of the Europeans and the South Pacific territories of the Americans. In order to rule Asia, these western powers would need to be neutralised.

As part of a strategy to deal the United States a serious blow, Japanese carrier-launched airplanes attacked Pearl Harbor in Hawaii on December 7, 1941. After the US declared war on Japan in response to the attack, Great Britain and her empire followed suit.

Already stretched and war weary after being at war for two years in Europe, Canada now had another front opened in the Pacific. Although only a footnote of the Second World War, this new front brought the war home to those on the West Coast.

1

Sunk! Japanese Submarine Warfare on the West Coast

SOME OF THE MOST INTRIGUING STORIES from the war on the West Coast are of Japan's submarines, the shadowy predators that struck and then vanished into the deep Pacific. Japan's largest submarines, dubbed "I-boats," were formidable undersea craft. At 108 metres long, they sported a 140-millimetre (5.5-inch) deck cannon, two 25-millimetre (one-inch) machine guns, and six 53-centimetre (21-inch) bow torpedo tubes. Carrying extra fuel, some had a cruising range of over 40,000 kilometres, more than ample for conducting a patrol to North America and back.

Forty-two of the I-boats had a watertight hangar forward of the conning-tower sail and were equipped to carry a collapsible, twin-pontoon float plane, the Yokosuka E14Y1,

Some Japanese submarines were equipped to carry an E14Y1 Glen airplane. I-25 launched its Glen over Oregon on two occasions.

which was dubbed "Glen" by the Allies. It could be assembled in 55 minutes by the ship's mechanics and was launched by a compressed-air catapult. When the aircraft returned from its mission and landed next to the sub, it was retrieved by a crane.

Some of the I-boats were fitted to carry a two-man midget submarine, the *Ko Hyoteki*, or up to six *Kaiten*, which were manned torpedoes. These one-man suicide craft were employed as Japan's Pacific fortunes crumbled under a relentless Allied siege and the Imperial Navy was reduced to desperately defending the homeland itself.

Despite its remarkable weaponry, the Japanese submarine force operated without one critical tool: surface radar. Before Japan acquired the technology in 1945, submarines lacking radar were easy pickings for American ships and planes with highly developed radar sets. The Allies had possessed the technology since the outbreak of the war.

Late in the war, Japan built the massive I-400 class of submarines, which were 122 metres in length and could carry three of the new Aichi M6A1 float fighter planes. This largest class of I-boat was never used to its full potential. As the war accelerated against Japan, much of Japan's submarine fleet was consigned to ferry troops and supplies between beleaguered outposts.

In December 1941, however, Japan's navy and army were enjoying phenomenal success, sweeping through the mid-Pacific and Asia. After the devastating attack on

Sunk!

Pearl Harbor, Admiral Isoroku Yamamoto, commander-in-chief of the combined Japanese naval forces, and the Imperial Navy were riding high on a wave of popularity. Admiral Yamamoto realized the aircraft carrier would replace the battleship as the dominant surface vessel. It was the lowly Swordfish aircraft launched from the British carrier *Ark Royal* that had brought about the destruction of the great German battleship *Bismarck*.

In the first months of the war, Yamamoto's faith in carrier warfare was borne out in victory after victory. Three days after the near-annihilation of the American Pacific battle fleet at Pearl Harbor, Japanese torpedo bombers sank the Royal Navy battleship *Prince of Wales* and the battle cruiser HMS *Repulse* near Singapore. In April 1942, 80 Japanese dive-bombers quickly sank two more Royal Navy heavy cruisers in the Indian Ocean. HMS *Dorsetshire* went down in eight minutes and HMS *Cornwall* in twelve minutes without the loss of a single Japanese plane.

In spite of these successes, Yamamoto was concerned about the very real threat of the American aircraft carriers that had eluded destruction at Pearl Harbor. Even with the Imperial Navy's meticulous planning, all had not gone according to plan on December 7. Prior to the attack, reconnaissance patrols over Pearl Harbor by submarine-launched aircraft had shown that the five aircraft carriers of the US Pacific Fleet were not tied up at the base, and subsequent patrols had failed to locate them. If they were not put out of commission, the Americans would still have a powerful presence in the Pacific. Following the attack, Yamamoto knew that the aircraft carriers were unlikely to return to Hawaii, which meant their probable destination was Australia or one of the mainland American bases: Los Angeles or San Francisco in California, the shipyards on the Columbia River in Oregon, or the Puget Sound naval facilities in Washington State. Japanese submarines fanned out from Hawaii in search of the carriers. Yamamoto immediately sent a force of nine submarines to North America's west coast, stationing them from off the west coast of Vancouver Island to San Diego.

The extensive US Navy support facilities in Puget Sound were of great interest to the Japanese. They believed the American carriers might be en route to these ports or already there. The Imperial Navy was well aware that all major marine traffic heading in or out of Puget Sound had one direct route to the Pacific—the Strait of Juan de Fuca, a 50-kilometre-wide body of water separating Vancouver Island and the Olympic Peninsula in Washington State.

Submarine I-25 was stationed off Juan de Fuca, patrolling as far south as the Columbia River, which separates Washington State and Oregon. The Columbia supported ship repair facilities and could handle deep-sea ships. There was also a large army installation at Fort Stevens, on the Oregon side, as well as a radar and radio-direction-finding station at the mouth of the river. Submarine I-26 patrolled from a point midway down Vancouver Island to Cape Flattery at the northwest tip of the Olympic Peninsula. Before Christmas of 1941, the submarines I-23, I-21, I-19, I-17, I-15, I-10 and I-9 had all taken up their positions off the coast.

Farther south, obvious targets were the waters from San Francisco to San Diego. All had major ports and large shipyards and saw a great deal of naval traffic. Los Angeles was the main US Navy base on the Pacific coast, while Santa Barbara was an important oil-producing area and a busy port for tanker ships. While the I-boats had been ordered to attack merchant ships when they were encountered, the primary goal of the West Coast offensive was the destruction of the American aircraft-carrier fleet.

The I-boats were also ordered to shell important shore facilities along the West Coast, such as navigational aids and military installations, which required them to move in close to the enemy shore. The Japanese had prior knowledge of many of these sites, including radar and radio-direction-finding posts, due to some creative intelligence gathering by the Imperial Navy. During the buildup of Japanese marine forces, many officers were drawn from the merchant service. Some were familiar with the West Coast ports because they had plied these waters during their careers. The Imperial Navy had also sent fishing vessels manned by navy sailors to reconnoiter the coast from Alaska to California. These ships likely deposited spies in West Coast ports prior to the war. The spies would have gathered information on shore defences and military installations, or the lack of them. Many first-generation

Japanese had settled along the coast, and they would readily welcome visitors from the homeland.

As part of their West Coast agenda, Japanese submarines shelled land targets in Hawaii, California, Oregon and British Columbia. Although they concentrated on military, transport and communications targets, the submarines had been ordered to shell coastal communities at midnight on Christmas Eve, 1941. All nine submarines were to surface at a predetermined time and bombard villages along the coast from British Columbia to California in a synchronized attack. This was strictly a terror tactic, targeting civilians rather than military or industrial sites and occurring on a holiday when businesses would be shut down and families at home. Japanese strategists believed that such a bombardment on the continent so soon after the attack at Pearl Harbor would weaken public morale and cause mass hysteria.

In the weeks leading up to the December 24 attack, the I-boats were busy. The lumber carrier *Samoa*, southbound with a cargo of timber from Washington State and headed for San Diego, was the first ship to come under attack along the West Coast shoreline. *Samoa*'s watch caught sight of the black shape of a submarine shadowing the freighter off Santa Barbara in the first light of December 18. The ship immediately began an evasive manoeuvre. Not wanting to lose his quarry, I-17's commander, Kuzo Nishino, hastily fired a torpedo at the retreating freighter. Halfway to the target, the torpedo exploded inexplicably—a sign of things to come for the I-boats. Nishino ordered his gun crew to shell the runaway ship. Of the five shells lobbed at the steamer before breaking off the attack, only one connected, inflicting minor damage on *Samoa*'s radio room. Later that evening, I-17 spotted the oil tanker *Emidio* southbound off northern California. Nishino moved to intercept the tanker on the surface but again was spotted by an alert watchman. Running on the surface, the enemy submarine quickly closed the gap between hunter and quarry to less than a thousand metres. The first mortar shot hit *Emidio*'s mid-ship cargo fuel tank, and the crew took to lifeboats, abandoning their doomed vessel. Ignoring the survivors, I-17 continued to shell the wallowing tanker, connecting with six more hits to ensure *Emidio*'s demise. A navy bomber en route to Seattle from San Francisco picked up *Emidio*'s mayday and caught the sub on the surface. One 135-kilogram (300-pound) anti-submarine bomb detonated perilously close to I-17, while a second bomb landed close enough to do damage but failed to explode. Nishino fired a single torpedo, which exploded under *Emidio*'s stern, then retreated from the area, believing the tanker was on its way to the bottom. Five members of *Emidio*'s crew died in the attack, and the hulk eventually washed onto the rocks at Crescent City, California, where it was declared a total loss. It remained hung up there until 1951.

On the afternoon of December 20, I-23 attacked the tanker *Agwiworld* off Santa Cruz Island. In a bold daylight surface attack, well within sight of the mainland, I-23 commander Genichi Shibata shot two 140-millimetre (5.5-inch) shells into the side of *Agwiworld*. First Officer Frederick Goncalves immediately took evasive manoeuvres and outran the sub to port, dodging eight more shells.

Two days later, Narahara Shogo's I-19 carried out a daylight surface attack. On a sunny December 22, I-19 surfaced off Point Arguello, 176 kilometres north of Los Angeles, to intercept the Standard Oil tanker *H.M. Storey*. In full view of beach strollers, I-19 landed several shells on the tanker. While *H.M. Storey* attempted to dodge the submarine's shells, Shogo fired four torpedoes; all missed their target or failed to detonate. Sure that patrols would have been alerted, Shogo broke off his attack and dived for cover. Although smoking, the tanker was able to make the safety of the tiny coastal resort community of Surf, California. Bombers arrived on the scene and peppered the area with anti-submarine bombs; however, I-19 was safely submerged and creeping south to patrol the waters off Los Angeles.

On December 23, one day before the planned bombardment of West Coast communities, the I-boats surfaced along the coast under cover of darkness to await further orders. The submarine commanders knew that the brazen strike directly at America would bring prestige to the Imperial Navy's submarine service. At the designated time for the message, around 2 A.M., the faint tapping of wireless sets on the enemy submarines from British Columbia to California brought a discouraging message. The commander of the Advance

Sunk!

Expeditionary Force—as the flotilla of subs operating on the West Coast was known—ordered that the Christmas bombardment was not to proceed. The admiralty was forced to concede that Japanese North Americans who populated some coastal areas might be killed during the attack and could also become targets of a severe backlash in retaliation for the attacks on civilians. The subs were ordered to maintain patrols and continue to seek out the enemy carriers.

Despite the unwelcome change in plans, the subs were not idle that day. I-17 made an unsuccessful attempt to shell the 7,000-ton freighter *Larry Doheny* 128 kilometres southwest of Los Angeles, but it inflicted only minor damage before the ship slipped into Long Beach harbour.

The tanker *Montebello*, its holds filled with crude oil, was outbound from Los Angeles and heading north for Vancouver, British Columbia, when Kanji Matsumura, on I-21, caught it in his sights off Monterey, California. In the early morning light, *Montebello*'s watch spotted the silhouette of a submarine shadowing them about a kilometre off the starboard quarter. Captain Olaf Eckstrom immediately put his vessel into an evasive pattern, but a torpedo struck directly under the starboard bridge, blowing off the deckhouse, radio room and forward mast. At once the ship began to settle by the bow, and Eckstrom ordered his crew away in lifeboats. Only minutes later, *Montebello* slipped under the waves. I-21 fired at the survivors, splintering the wooden lifeboats but miraculously missing all of the 36 crewmen, all of whom survived the attack. In 1997, *Montebello* was discovered in 250 metres of water, less than two kilometres off the marine ecological reserve at Monterey Bay.

Withdrawing south from the *Montebello* sinking, I-21 came across the tanker *Idaho* off California's Long Beach and took up pursuit, firing several rounds that all missed their target. *Idaho* managed to elude Matsumura long enough to escape into the safety of Long Beach's harbour.

The following morning, Shogo, in I-19, spotted the freighter *Barbara Olsen* off Long Beach and lined her up for a torpedo attack. Again his torpedoes failed him, exploding short of the freighter. The alerted ship's crew outran the sub into Long Beach, and a frustrated Shogo recorded four more torpedoes fired and four more misses. Shogo moved I-19 into Catalina Channel off Point Fermin, and later that same day he spied the lumber freighter *Absaroka* heading south. He fired two torpedoes. The first officer ticked off the minutes on his stopwatch, shaking his head when time ran out on the first fish. As time clicked down on the second torpedo, the sharp rattle of an explosion reverberated through the sub's hull. Raising the periscope, Shogo could see *Absaroka* had taken the hit amidships and was already settling in the water. He was lining up *Absaroka* for another shot when a patrol plane appeared, forcing him to dive before he could get off a parting shot. The freighter, buoyed by her cargo of lumber, was towed to Bethlehem Shipyards in San Francisco and repaired.

In Monterey Bay, the armed yacht *Dorothy Philips* was

outbound on Christmas Eve when I-23 opened fire. No match for a 109-metre submarine, the little gunboat sped back toward the bay and ran aground on the approaches. The sub, however, had given up the chase.

The appearance of enemy submarines off the coast in the frantic weeks following the attack on Pearl Harbor set everyone on edge. In 1941 and 1942, 147 submarine sightings were reported along the coast from the Columbia River to southern Alaska, and anti-submarine patrols were often needlessly sent out to investigate, which strained valuable resources and put crews at risk. Anxious comrades watched the hours pass as patrol planes failed to return in the wretched weather of northern BC and Alaska. Occasionally, an over-anxious aircrew bombed a submarine only to discover that the target was an unfortunate whale.

Japanese submariners contributed to the confusion by releasing hundreds of dummy periscopes, which consisted of a buoyed bamboo pole with a weight at one end to hold the "periscope" upright. The Canadian army's heavy guns successfully "sank" one of these ersatz submarines off Gordon Head near Victoria in January 1941. This ruse kept Allied anti-submarine forces on useless search-and-destroy missions long after the I-boats had withdrawn from the West Coast. It also partially explains the disproportionately high number of submarine sightings and anti-submarine attacks recorded along the coast compared to the small number of enemy subs actually deployed there.

In February 1942, I-17 was back on the prowl in American waters. This time, Captain Nishino intended to bomb the oil installations along the shores of Santa Barbara Channel at Goleta. Under the cover of a predawn sky, Nishino guided his boat to scout the installations, approaching so closely that he could see the vehicle headlights moving along the Pacific Highway. He then waited for nightfall to make his attack. For 10 hours, the crew whiled away the time, drinking hot tea and playing cards in the submerged boat. At 7:00 P.M., Nishino brought his submarine back to the surface and ordered a three-man gun crew to station on the 140-millimetre (5.5-inch) gun. I-17 then fired 17 shells into the oil-pumping station in a brazen strike at America. These were the first enemy shells to fall on the continent since the War of 1812. Fearing entrapment by anti-submarine forces between the Channel Islands and the mainland, the sub dived and proceeded north. There was minor damage on the shore, and one US artillery-man was injured while deactivating an unexploded shell. He would be the only serviceman injured by enemy action on the continental US during the war and was awarded the Purple Heart for his injuries.

The following day, bold headlines in the *Los Angeles Times* and *Examiner* newspapers reported the bombing of the Los Angeles area by Japanese aircraft. Others reported that the town of Santa Barbara itself was bombarded by enemy planes and cruisers. That night, jittery anti-aircraft batteries around Los Angeles fired off 1,700 rounds of ammunition at flocks of birds and imagined enemy bombers. The physical damage I-17 had caused amounted to about $500, but the propaganda wrought by media in North America caused a different sort of damage, stoking the embers of distrust against Japanese North Americans.

Nishino made one more attack before he left the West Coast. On March 1, 1942, I-17 was in the waters off San Francisco's Golden Gate. Troop carrier *William H. Berg* was returning to San Francisco when I-17 sent a torpedo under the ship's aft end. The submarine surfaced to attack with gunfire, but the troopship fired back from deck-mounted guns. Nishino quickly dived, surprised at the quick reaction from the American crew, and hastily left American waters. *William H. Berg* sustained no damage.

Captain Emi Tetsushiro, the commander of I-8, was anxious to record a kill on the West Coast but had lurked off Juan de Fuca Strait for a month with nothing to show for it. During his time on the West Coast, Canadian anti-submarine patrols reported sightings in the Juan de Fuca area. Watchmen on the minesweeper HMCS *Outarde* spotted a submarine periscope in their wake, but when they turned on the target they came up empty-handed.

That same month, as a twin-engine Bolingbroke from No. 8 Bomber-Reconnaissance Squadron was returning to base at Sea Island, near Vancouver, aircrew observed a submarine break the surface a kilometre astern of their aircraft. When the plane banked for an attack, the submarine immediately dived and escaped the bombs dropped on the area.

The *Moolack*, a tug consigned to the Fishermen's Volunteer Reserve (FVR), was towing a barge of explosives into the Strait of Juan de Fuca when it reported that a periscope had surfaced between the tug and its tow. The periscope immediately retracted as the barge closed over the site. An inexperienced watch officer on duty ordered the tug, unarmed and without any means of searching for a submerged submarine, to drop its tow and attack the submarine, much to the alarm of the tug's seasoned crew. After animated radio discussion, experience and common sense prevailed. In the fog and currents of the strait, a loose barge could easily end up on the rocks or collide with another vessel, which would have given Tetsushiro a kill in a very roundabout manner. I-8 left for Kure, Japan, without a single attack on an Allied vessel.

With the unreliability of early Japanese torpedoes, hunting off the West Coast proved a disappointment to the submariners. No aircraft carriers or major warships had been spotted along the coast, let alone attacked and sunk, and Allied anti-submarine patrols were better prepared and reacted more quickly than the I-boats' skippers had expected. Still, the Japanese submariners gained a noteworthy status amongst their comrades. They had brought the Pacific war to the very shores of North America.

2

Minoru Yakota
and I-26

AMONG THE NINE SUBMARINES THAT patrolled North America's west coast, Captain Minoru Yakota's I-26 would make the greatest mark on Canadian history. In June 1942, Yakota launched the first enemy attack on Canadian soil since the War of 1812.

Yakota's war had begun several months earlier on December 7, 1941, the day of the Pearl Harbor attacks. Out in the great expanse of the Pacific Ocean between North America and Hawaii, the steamer *Cynthia Olson* slowly made her way from Seattle to Hawaii with her cargo of dressed lumber. Although far from the danger at Pearl Harbor, *Cynthia Olson* would soon be the first American casualty on the West Coast, and the first kill by Minoru Yakota.

Yakota was running his submarine's electric motors at flank speed on a course that would intercept the little steamship. Taking his eyes from the periscope sight, he made note of the time: 3:19 A.M., Tokyo time. Within 19 minutes, Admiral Isoroku Yamamoto's carrier force would strike at Pearl Harbor. Once the massive attack was underway, I-26 could fire on *Cynthia Olson*. Until then, Yakota could only watch and wait.

Yakota chose to approach the steamer submerged in order to put his green crew through some practice attacks. As I-26 had completed its sea trials only two months earlier, the new crew had not had time to polish its skills in submarine warfare. Compounding this lack of experience was dubious weaponry. Yakota's boat was the last to receive its stock of munitions and had been allotted only 10 outdated torpedoes of questionable reliability.

Again Yakota glanced at his wristwatch: 3:30 A.M., Tokyo time. He waited five more minutes and then gave the order to surface. On deck, Chief Gunner Saburo Hayashi's gun crew hoisted the firing block into the gun breech and loaded one shell into the 140-millimetre (5.5-inch) deck cannon. The warning shot whistled across *Cynthia Olson*'s bow, but the crew did not respond, and the steamer casually followed its original course. After a second warning shot, *Cynthia Olson*'s crew noticed and heaved to. Yakota allowed the crew time to abandon ship in two lifeboats before opening fire with the deck gun. Despite taking shots for several hours, *Cynthia Olson*, buoyed by its cargo of lumber, did not sink. After a torpedo aimed at the steamer missed its mark, Yakota submerged his boat to hide from any American planes that might be on their way.

During the time allowed to abandon ship, *Cynthia Olson's* wireless operator had alerted the Matson liner *Lurline*, 600 kilometres to the south, that they were under attack by submarine. *Lurline* relayed the SOS to San Francisco. For some unexplained reason, the initial reports of the Pearl Harbor attack didn't come in until 55 minutes later. *Cynthia Olson's* SOS was North America's first notice of war in the Pacific.

After 35 minutes Yakota ordered I-26 to resurface to fire more rounds into *Cynthia Olson*. After seven hours, with the doomed ship about to sink and no American aircraft in sight, I-26 headed northeast toward Washington State and British Columbia.

After drifting for several days, *Cynthia Olson's* survivors were spotted by another Japanese submarine, I-19, which stopped to render medical and navigational assistance. This act of compassion was in contravention of the edict issued by the commander of the First Submarine Flotilla to kill all enemy survivors. In spite of I-19's efforts, *Cynthia Olson's* crew was lost in the Pacific Ocean and never seen again.

On June 7, 1942, Minoru Yakota's I-26 lay in wait at the mouth of the Strait of Juan de Fuca, hoping to intercept any American aircraft carriers that had been docked at Seattle. The overall Japanese plan called for an air strike against Alaska

Commander Minoru Yakota of submarine I-26 sank the first American vessel of the Pacific war. He made two patrols of the Pacific Northwest. CHARLES AIKENS

at Dutch Harbor in an attempt to draw out the US aircraft carriers. When they moved north to defend Alaska, they would have to pass within range of I-26.

Shortly past noon on June 7, Coastwise Steamship Line's *Coast Trader*, bound from Port Angeles to San Francisco, came into view of Yakota's periscope, 40 kilometres southwest of Port Renfrew on Vancouver Island. Following the freighter at periscope depth, Yakota closed to within 750 metres of the freighter. He sounded off co-ordinates to his senior torpedo man as he manoeuvred his submarine into attack position. *Coast Trader* glided into Yakota's co-ordinates, and he was ready to fire. On Yakota's command two torpedoes were fired, followed minutes later by two terrific explosions on *Coast Trader's* port side. Aboard the freighter, ruptured steam lines filled the engine room with burning, choking vapours. The sea immediately flowed in through buckled hull plates and busted valves, dousing the engines and generators.

Verne Wilkert, a 20-year-old who had just signed on as an oiler, was knocked out when he was blown headfirst against a steel bulkhead by the enormous blast. When he came to, he was in total darkness, immersed in diesel fuel and water. His head still reeling from the impact, he found a ladder and hung on. He figured he was done for, but then he saw daylight above him. The impact had knocked the blackout screen off the ventilation shaft. Pulling himself through the duct and onto the listing deck, Wilkert struggled into a life jacket and slipped over the side into the cold water. The ship was aflame and settling at the stern, and debris littered the oily water. Wilkert slipped in and out of consciousness as fellow sailors grappled him into a lifeboat. When he awoke, *Coast Trader* had already disappeared. All 36 crewmen managed to get away safely to lifeboats, but one died during the night from burns and exposure. Wilkert's lifeboat was rescued by the fishing vessel *Virginia I* and towed into the Native reservation at Neah Bay near Cape Flattery. The following morning, the Canadian corvette HMCS *Edmunston* picked up two more life rafts with survivors and discharged them at Port Angeles. *Edmunston* and aircraft from Sidney, BC, and Washington carried out a systematic search for the enemy submarine but found no trace of it. Yakota had already made his way north to wait out the hunt off Vancouver Island's Barkley Sound.

Yakota continued to prowl the west coast of Vancouver Island and was proceeding on a northerly course eight kilometres off Barkley Sound. At dawn, the sub had been forced to dive after the fishing vessel *Talapus*, a member of the FVR, spotted it from about six kilometres astern. In fact, *Talapus*'s crew did not realize they were following a submarine until it dived, as its silhouette resembled another FVR vessel, *Marauder*. After several hours, Yakota resurfaced and continued north. It was almost the longest day of the year, so at 10 P.M., the setting sun still illuminated the western horizon.

I-boats patrolling the West Coast had orders to shell important shore-based installations as well as ships. Aware of a radar and radio-direction-finding installation beyond the Estevan Point Lighthouse, which now lay to starboard of I-26, Yakota decided to shell it. The submarines had orders to destroy these direction-finding locators, as they could home in on the submarines' radio transmissions.

By 10:17 P.M. on June 20, the sky to the west still cast its fading light over Hesquiat, the Nuu-chah-nulth village nestled behind Estevan Point's lighthouse. Yakota, standing atop the conning tower, ordered Chief Gunner Saburo Hayashi to commence firing with the 140-millimetre (5.5-inch) gun. The first shell landed 550 metres short of the lighthouse and sent up six-metre geysers of water. Yakota scolded the crew to aim higher. Several more shells landed around the lighthouse as the gun crew adjusted the range. Following shots went high over the Nuu-chah-nulth village, landing in a hilly area beyond the community. As the shells exploded, lights were doused in the tiny village and the gun crew could hear the frantic squealing of pigs.

On shore, wireless operator Edward T. Redford radioed "We are being shelled!" Shells were missing the lighthouse but landing all around the village five kilometres away. Lighthouse keeper Robert Lally hurled himself up the spiral staircase of the tower to douse the thousand-watt light that had been kept burning in spite of submarine threats because of the treacherous waters off Vancouver Island's west coast. From his vantage point, Lally logged the second and third salvoes, noting that they exploded with such force the lighthouse tower shook and three of the lantern windows were taken out by flying debris. I-26 got off about 21 shots before Yakota ordered the submarine away, having done little other than alert the enemy to his presence.

An air-force bomber peeled down the airstrip at Patricia Bay, but spun out, cracking up and blocking the runway so no other craft could take off. It was 30 minutes before an aircraft from Coal Harbour, near Port Hardy, flew over the area, but it turned up nothing.

I-26 remained off BC's coast until mid-July and returned to Yokosuka via the Aleutians without finding any more targets. Yakota's actions finally caused lighthouses along the West Coast to be blacked out, causing the Russian freighter *Uzbekistan* to crash onto the rocks at Pachena Point with a load of Lend-Lease materials in April 1943.

3

Meiji Tagami
and I-25

CAPTAIN MEIJI TAGAMI, COMMANDER OF I-25, would become the most renowned of the enemy submariners, conducting three patrols off the shores of North America. On his first patrol, Tagami took up station off the mouth of the Columbia River on December 18, 1941. Sometime after midnight, Tagami spied the outline of a merchant ship off Destruction Point on the Washington coast. It was the Union Oil tanker *L.P. St. Clair*, running from the Pacific Northwest to the oil facilities at Santa Barbara. The tanker was crossing the mouth of the river when Tagami ordered his crew to open fire with the deck cannon. When the first rounds sent up geysers of water alongside *L.P. St. Clair*, skipper John Ellison ordered an abrupt course change that took him into the river.

He knew the sub was unlikely to follow him there. I-25 fired 10 rounds, all of which missed, before *L.P. St. Clair* made it into the safety of the Columbia River.

By December 27, 1941, only I-25 remained on the West Coast. The other submarines had withdrawn to the Japanese base at Kwajalein in the Marshall Islands to resupply or to picket the waters around Hawaii. Tagami, still patrolling off Oregon that December day, attacked the petroleum tanker *Connecticut*, which was well into the Columbia River. This was a bold move as the area was populated and defended by 203-millimetre (8-inch) guns installed at Fort Stevens at the mouth of the river.

Fort Stevens had been established during the American Civil War to counter the sizable Royal Navy presence in Victoria, British Columbia. The Americans feared the British or Confederates might try to seize territory at the mouth of the Columbia while the Union Army was occupied fighting the Confederate forces. This gave Fort Stevens the distinction of being the only Civil War fort west of the Missouri River.

Tagami struck *Connecticut* with a single torpedo. In the ensuing chase, the tanker ran hard aground on a sandbar, taking on a port list as the tide receded. Believing the ship was sinking, Tagami withdrew and left the Oregon coast. Miraculously, the torpedo did not ignite the tanker's explosive cargo, and the ship was later salvaged from the Columbia River bar that had kept it from sinking.

By January 11, 1942, Tagami withdrew to Kwajalein via Hawaii to resupply. In February 1942 the sub was ordered to patrol the waters of Australia and New Zealand. In Australia, Tagami brazenly launched I-25's Glen reconnaissance plane over Sydney, Melbourne and Hobart, unchallenged by Allied aircraft. The sub patrolled the south Pacific Ocean until April when it returned for refit at the Yokosuka Navy Yard in Japan.

In May, I-25 and I-26 sailed for Alaska by way of the Aleutian Islands; I-25 launched its Glen float plane over the US Navy anchorage at Kodiak Island and reported only minor navy vessels. After scouting Kodiak and Dutch Harbor, Tagami's I-25 and Minoru Yakota's I-26 headed south to Cape Flattery. Their mission was to report on any major warship movements coming out of the Strait of Juan de Fuca.

While I-25 was travelling south, several witnesses, including the lighthouse keeper, spotted it off Langara Island in the Queen Charlotte Islands (now Haida Gwaii). Some local people were evacuated but others remained to keep watch on the I-boat. After some time, the boat submerged without incident.

Eventually a US Coast Guard cutter and the FVR vessel *Moolack* arrived to carry out a cursory search for the submarine. At the time, many unfounded reports of submarines were being made; most sightings were likely whales, fishing boats or logs. In this case, however, witnesses told a shore party from the vessels that the sub had remained on the surface for some time before diving and that it was unmistakably a submarine. Years later, Tagami confirmed that his boat had been spotted off Langara Island and that he had dived, assuming aircraft had been alerted.

I-25 made its way to the Cape Flattery area of Washington State by mid-June. Tagami had been running on the surface under cover of darkness to recharge the sub's batteries and compressed-air cylinders. Just after midnight on June 20, I-25's watch caught sight of the freighter *Fort Camosun*. The ship had just been built at Victoria Machinery Depot for the British Ministry of Transport and was headed south on its maiden voyage to Europe via the Panama Canal with a load of lumber and raw materials for the war effort. Within a couple of hours, Tagami had lined up the 7,100-ton freighter and fired a single torpedo that ripped *Fort Camosun*'s hull on the port side. Two holds immediately filled with water, flooding the engines, auxiliary generators and steam-powered motors as the ship began to settle evenly in the water. Half-dressed crewmen, wakened by the shock of the explosion, spilled into darkened passageways, yelling, "Torpedo! Torpedo!"

As crewmen pulled away in lifeboats, a shell whistled over the freighter's bow. A second landed in her side, opening up the hull. Fearing aircraft had been alerted, Tagami dived and broke off the attack. *Fort Camosun* actually had managed to get off a distress call, but the nearest help—the Canadian corvettes *Edmunston* and *Quesnel*—was six hours away. As dawn broke, the two corvettes found the stricken freighter swamped, her main deck nearly awash but held afloat by her cargo of lumber. Tagami had returned to the scene and shot up his scope for a quick look at the rescue attempt. HMCS *Quesnel* detected the sounds of the submarine and began laying depth charges to force the I-boat away while *Edmunston* picked up two lifeboats of survivors and began salvage operations. HMCS *Vancouver* and the American armed yacht *Y-994* arrived later to join in the search for the submarine, but by noon it had been lost.

When the Canadian salvage tug *Dauntless* and US Navy tug *Tatnuck* arrived in the late afternoon, they found *Edmunston* struggling to tow *Fort Camosun* to safety in a rising sea, the freighter's main deck only a few feet above water. Late the following day, as the ships rounded Cape Flattery, it was decided to beach *Fort Camosun* at Neah Bay on the American side. As waves began breaking over *Fort Camosun* and it settled lower in the water, all four vessels were overwhelmed while trying to keep a handle on the unwieldy tow. After reaching the safety of the bay, temporary repairs were made and the tug *Canadian National 2* arrived and towed *Fort Camosun* to the dock at Victoria, where a large piece of a Japanese torpedo was discovered in the twisted metal.

Fort Camosun, built at Victoria, BC, was on its maiden voyage when it was attacked by I-25. It is shown here under tow following the attack. VANCOUVER MARITIME MUSEUM

The next day, Tagami and his crew again readied to attack American soil from the Columbia River. His submarine slipped through homebound fishboats to within eight kilometres of Cape Disappointment, which marks the river's entrance. Sometime before midnight, he brought I-25 to the surface and lined the submarine up, deck cannon facing directly aft and bow pointing to open sea.

Tagami gave the order to fire the 140-millimetre (5.5-inch) cannon, landing the first shots in front of Battery Russell, which was off active duty that night. The explosions broke the sleep of the soldiers sleeping in tents behind the battery, and confusion reigned as the men ran about in their undershorts, the darkness lit up by exploding mortars. Several observation posts, as well as the armed yacht *Manana II*, radioed alarms to the fort's control centre, which by then was well aware of the shelling.

Along the beach in front of the fort was a string of observation posts manned with searchlights and machine guns. The farthest post was eight kilometres from the main fort. An exploding shell cut the telephone line connecting the fort to the three northernmost beach posts. When the control centre at Fort Stevens was unable to raise these posts, it assumed the Japanese had landed, cut the communication lines and captured the placements.

I-25's position would have been less than five kilometres from shore, directly in line with the wreck of *Peter Iredale* on the beach. The fire-control centre at Fort Stevens calculated the sub was out of range of the battery's big guns, so it never gave the order to fire or even turn on the searchlights. This was an odd assumption, since the submarine's comparatively small gun had a range of only eight kilometres and was landing shells on the shore. For Tagami, it proved a fortunate error in judgment. He later wrote that he would never have risked his ship or the lives of the 108 sailors aboard if he'd had any idea of the number and size of guns aimed in his direction. The sub's gunner estimated that he fired 17 shots in the direction of the fort.

On Delaura Beach Road, a shell landed metres short of a home owned by the Hitchmen family, splintering a tree and leaving a three-metre crater in Mrs. Hitchmen's garden. Another shot sailed over the house and exploded just outside the new cemetery about a kilometre inland. Then Tagami retreated north, slipping past the blacked-out shapes of *Manana II* and the *Columbia* lightship, leaving the onshore confusion behind.

By June 27, I-25 had made its way north and was again patrolling the waters around Dutch Harbor, Alaska. The return trip proved uneventful, and after a brief call into the Japanese-held Alaskan island of Kiska, it headed to Yokosuka Navy Yard for replenishment. On August 15, Tagami departed Yokosuka, arriving once again off Oregon in early September for his third patrol of the West Coast. He claimed that one torpedo hit an unidentified ship. For three weeks, the submarine's objective was to launch the Glen over Oregon, and it achieved two successful flights over the coast with pilot Nobuo Fujita and observer Okuda Shoji.

On October 4, while patrolling Oregon's southern coastline about 80 kilometres west of Coos Bay, Tagami spotted the 6,600-ton tanker *Camden* sitting dead in the water. Loaded with 76,000 barrels of gasoline, it had suffered a serious mechanical problem and been forced to shut down its engines. Tagami lined up the tanker and fired two torpedoes. The first passed astern of the ship, but the second slammed into its side and erupted into a wall of flames. Civilian and military ships came to *Camden*'s rescue and brought the fire under control before towing it toward Seattle. But the fire continued to burn, and on October 10 it again raged out of control and engulfed the ship. *Camden* sank off Gray's Harbor, six days after being torpedoed.

Still lurking off Oregon's southern coast, Tagami came upon the tanker *Larry Doheny*, loaded with 66,000 barrels of oil. *Larry Doheny* regularly transported oil between Santa Barbara and Puget Sound, and had escaped an attack by I-17 in December 1941. Racing on the dark surface to intercept the unsuspecting ship, Tagami ordered one torpedo launched, but it petered out by the time it hit the target and failed to detonate. *Larry Doheny* steamed on, unaware it was being lined up for a torpedo attack. Tagami ordered a second torpedo fired, and the submarine's crew fell silent and listened as it made its way to the target. A tremendous explosion echoed back to I-25, confirming a hit.

Above, the tanker became an inferno and sank the next day as rescue crews stood by. Forty men made it to lifeboats while six others died in the attack. Escaping to safety, Tagami decided to end their third patrol to the West Coast. The submarine had been the target of a surprise attack a month before that left a telltale trail of oil, and they were down to their last torpedo.

As Tagami headed northwest about 1,200 kilometres off the Washington–British Columbia coastline on October 11, his soundman alerted him to the noises of two distant ships. Tagami followed the sounds to two submarines, which he assumed to be American. He switched to silent running on electric motors and positioned his boat so the targets would pass nearby. Then he fired his last torpedo. The resulting explosion was so severe it shattered gauges, light bulbs and the porcelain toilets aboard his own sub.

Unknown to Tagami, the submarine hit was L-16 of the Soviet navy's Pacific fleet, en route to the Panama Canal with sister sub L-15. The sub sank in 20 seconds with all hands, and L-15 immediately opened fire on I-25, while taking evasive action. Despite their belief that they had sunk an American enemy, there was no joy aboard I-25 as they knew it was unlikely there would be survivors. After the gruelling 70-day patrol, I-25 pulled into Yokosuka in November 1942. It was not until 1973, 31 years later, that Tagami learned of L-16's identity and nationality.

4

The Man
Who Bombed America

CANADA'S ENTRY INTO THE Second World War in September 1939 had brought little change to the daily routine of West Coast citizens; life went on pretty much as it had during peacetime. Merchant ships made no attempt to conceal their courses, lighthouses continued to shine their beacons and coastal communities followed no blackout procedures. Yet, although the war seemed far removed from this peaceful coast, danger threatened from offshore.

Japanese submarine I-25 conducted the most frequent patrols of any Japanese submarine off the west coast of North America. In two previous tours it had ranged from Oregon to the Gulf of Alaska, Kodiak Island and the Aleutian Islands. In the summer of 1942, it was back in the

Pacific Northwest with a new mission. In its deck hangar, the submarine carried a Glen collapsible aircraft for reconnaissance purposes. Warrant Officer Nobuo Fujita had used it before in reconnoitering Sydney and Hobart, Australia, and over Woman's Bay on Kodiak Island. Fujita thought that this little plane could be used for more covert missions and deployed in numbers to attack the West Coast cities of North America.

Fujita had promoted his plan to Imperial Navy headquarters and was surprised when, during a refit of the I-25 at Yokosuka Navy Yard, he was summoned to the flotilla offices. There he met with Prince Takamatsu, the younger brother of Emperor Hirohito, and Commander Shojiro Iura of the 3rd Division Submarines. Iura was the former Japanese vice-consul, who until the war had been posted in Seattle, Washington.

Prince Takamatsu endorsed the idea, and the Imperial headquarters approved it. Fujita was told he was to bomb the American mainland. He was thrilled that the Imperial Navy had singled out his idea and that he would be the one to execute the mission. Using US Hydrographic Survey charts captured from American sources in Asia, Commander Iura indicated an area about 120 kilometres north of the California border in Oregon and approximately 16 kilometres inland. This was where Fujita was to bomb the forests. Fujita was disappointed; he had hoped to strike at a major city and didn't see the sense of dropping his bombs on a forest.

The consul explained that the Pacific Northwest was full of trees, and once a fire got started, it was very hard to put out. The reasoning was that the Americans would panic if they knew Japan could bomb "their country, their factories and homes." Realizing that this was to be the first of many such missions to strike directly at the mainland, an elated Fujita returned to his submarine.

On August 14, I-25 left Yokosuka, arriving off the Cape Blanco lighthouse on Oregon's southern coast on September 2. Seven days of inclement weather made launching the Glen impossible. The sub surfaced at night to recharge its batteries and dived before first light to rest on the shallow banks off the Oregon lighthouse.

Early in the morning of September 9, his submarine still jostled by waves, Commander Tagami viewed the Oregon coast from periscope depth and made the decision to attack. He called Fujita to have a look. Sixteen kilometres in the distance was the lighthouse of Cape Blanco. Tagami ordered the sub to the surface and the watertight hangar opened for assembly of the Glen aircraft. Two 75-kilogram (165-pound) incendiary bombs, each containing 520 pellets of highly combustible magnesium, were loaded onto the aircraft. Upon ignition, the pellets would burn at a temperature of 1,500°C and cover an area over 100 metres in diameter.

As Fujita and observer Shoji Okuda climbed into the plane, Commander Tagami wished them well. Fujita revved the single engine, gave the thumbs up, and the compressed-air catapult fired the little plane off the submarine deck. I-25 quickly slipped under the waves.

Heading toward Oregon, Fujita passed over Gold Beach and climbed to about 2,500 metres. A dairy farmer spotted the unusual plane with its Japanese red sun markings over Port Orford and phoned the sighting to the US Coast Guard, which responded with disbelief and hung up. Soon the dense coniferous rainforest of Oregon appeared. After about 30 minutes, Fujita and Okuda released the first of their incendiaries over Wheeler Ridge. The bomb hurled to earth, spinning end over end, splitting a tree and spilling the magnesium pellets onto the forest floor. Fujita and Okuda noted they ignited like fireworks and burst into flames. After a few minutes, Fujita released the second bomb. In a small way, this was his personal retaliation for an attack the previous February, when Colonel James Doolittle's B-25s bombed Tokyo and the Yokosuka base, punching a hole in I-25 while it sat in dry dock. The second of the two bombs apparently failed to ignite, as neither of the two men could see any sign of fire below. To this day, beneath the deep forest of Wheeler Ridge, the 75-kilogram (165-pound) incendiary bomb still lies unexploded.

To the northeast, forest rangers at the Mount Emily Firewatch Station noticed the unusual float plane, noted it in the daily logbook and made passing mention of it in their morning call to forestry headquarters. A soldier coming off duty reported the unidentified plane as it headed out to sea at about 6:30 A.M. in the Cape Blanco area. The Roseburg Filter Centre, which collected all information regarding enemy activity in the area, now started to seriously consider the idea that some enemy activity was taking place. A squadron of P-38 Lightning fighters was scrambled from McChord Field near Tacoma, but flew in the wrong direction due to a soldier's strong southern accent. His reference to Bandon was taken to mean the town of Bend, Oregon.

Later that day, forestry workers discovered a patch of small, sporadic fires covering an area about 30 metres across. Sifting through the site, they found unlit incendiary pellets, metal fragments and the nose cone of a bomb with Japanese markings. When it hit the tree, the bomb failed to fully detonate, so the fires were contained to a small area.

American officials saw the bombing as a prelude to invasion and ordered small infantry units dispatched up and down the Pacific Coast Highway, although they had antiquated battle gear and only five to ten rounds of ammunition per man. One of the only truly effective measures the units could take was to remove road signs along the highway so that if the enemy did land amphibiously on Oregon's beaches, it would take longer for them to find their way to population centres.

While the bombs caused little material damage, they did create anxiety in certain quarters. Some of the military brass believed the Japanese had smuggled pontooned aircraft to remote lakes, where they would assemble them and then bomb American cities. Special FBI agents spent weeks on horseback scouting the wilderness areas but found nothing.

Fujita and Okuda made it safely back to the rendezvous point with I-25 and dismantled and stowed the Glen in the hangar. They were just about to go below decks when the lookout shouted, pointing to the sky. Out of the sun roared a twin-engine Lockheed Hudson piloted by Captain Jean Daugherty, who was on routine patrol out of McChord Field when he spotted the enemy sub. Armed with two 135-kilogram (300-pound) bombs, he went in for the kill just as I-25 cleared the surface. The first bomb detonated next to the sub and sent it rolling sharply to starboard, plunging the crew into darkness. With water seeping into the radio room, Commander Tagami ordered the boat into a crash dive.

Daugherty banked around to drop the other bomb, and it exploded over the top of the submarine with a shock that rattled the submariners' teeth as the boat continued its dive before levelling off at around 30 metres. Tagami ordered the electric motors off, and the boat drifted along with the current while each station reported its damage. Several hours later, after ascertaining that the damage was minimal, Tagami ordered the electric motors engaged and to proceed dead slow. Silently, the submarine entered the harbour of Port Orford and settled on the bottom. It remained there until nightfall, giving the crew time to rest and repair damage.

Nobuo Fujita twice bombed Oregon from his E14Y1 Glen aircraft. It was the only enemy bombing by aircraft of the continental United States during the Second World War.
CHARLES AIKEN

For nearly three weeks, I-25 kept a low profile, but in the early-morning darkness of September 29, Fujita and Okuda readied the plane for a second bombing mission over Oregon. Again the I-boat took up position about 80 kilometres off the Cape Blanco lighthouse and catapulted the Glen off the submarine deck. After flying inland for half an hour, Fujita dropped two incendiaries into the forest 11 kilometres east of Port Orford. Noting the flashes as the bombs disappeared into the dense bush, he believed he had ignited a forest fire. Once again, forest rangers sighted the plane and reported it to the Roseburg Filter Centre, but search and fire crews found no evidence of fire or incendiaries.

Fujita made it back out to sea and circled the rendezvous point, but there was no sign of I-25. As his compass had on occasion been inaccurate, he returned to the coast to take a new heading off the Cape Blanco lighthouse. Spotting an oil slick on the water, he followed it and in a short time saw the black outline of I-25 running partially submerged. The two airmen made it aboard, and Fujita reported to Tagami that there were several fires burning out of control. But this was only wishful thinking; due to an unusually wet September in 1942, any fire started by Fujita and Okuda would have burned itself out quickly.

Taking a page from Fujita's exploits, Japan developed the massive I-400 class of submarine. Carrying three advanced Aichi M6A Seiran fighter planes, the submarines were ready to attack the Panama Canal, Los Angeles and New York, but the war ended before these plans were carried out. In his lowly Glen, Fujita remains the only man who bombed America.

5

War Comes to Alaska: The Battle of Dutch Harbor

WHILE IMPERIAL NAVY SUBMARINES WERE patrolling West Coast waters to the south, Japan was engaging the US in a deadly contest in Alaska, led by Admiral Isoroku Yamamoto, commander-in-chief of Japan's naval forces. Yamamoto had been the architect of the Pearl Harbor attack, which was designed to destroy the US aircraft carrier fleet. But the US carriers, located in waters south of Hawaii, had escaped destruction, and subsequent Japanese submarine patrols off Hawaii, North America and Australia had failed to find and destroy them. Consequently, the United States remained a powerful opponent in the Pacific.

In response to the threat posed by the Americans, Yamamoto and his admirals devised a twofold plan. Japan would initiate a carrier-launched attack on Alaska at Dutch Harbor, a fishing village in the eastern Aleutian Islands. An assault force would then occupy Attu and Kiska in the west of the chain, Adak, at its centre, and Dutch Harbor itself. When the aircraft carriers of the US fleet steamed north to defend Alaska, they would be met and destroyed by a Japanese force. Midway, located 2,200 kilometres north of Hawaii, was a minor US possession supporting a garrison of Marines and an assortment of fighter planes. Japan had long desired this Pacific atoll, an important base from which it could stage an invasion of Hawaii.

Thus the attack on Alaska would finish off the US Pacific fleet and put Japan in control of Midway. It would also ensure Japan was not threatened by enemy bases in the Aleutians and would cut the northern supply route from North America to Russia. Japanese bases in the Aleutians could be used as staging points for direct action against North America, and Japanese warships would be free to harass the West Coast. Long-range bombers could hit the Boeing aircraft plants and shipyards located at Seattle and Vancouver. Once cities along the West Coast had been bombed, the American desire to hold on to its South Pacific territories would be greatly diminished—certainly the American public would want to negotiate peace with Japan, and the United States would be forced to cede control of the western Pacific.

Early in 1942, Yamamoto was told to proceed with his Midway/Aleutian plan. The starting date for the ambitious campaign was set for early June, and a squadron of warships was dispatched to Dutch Harbor. The aircraft carriers *Ryujo* and *Junyo* sailed with the heavy cruisers *Takao* and *Maya* and a screen of three destroyers, *Akebono*, *Ushio* and *Sazanami*, as well as fleet oiler *Teiyo Maru* and a vanguard of submarines. Below decks, *Ryujo* carried 16 Mitsubishi Zeros and 21 Nakajima "Kate" light bombers, while *Junyo*, Japan's newest carrier, had 24 Zeros and 21 Aichi "Val" dive-bombers. Commanded by Rear Admiral Kakuji Kakuta, the squadron was the Second Carrier Striking Force and part of Admiral Boshiro Hosogaya's Northern Striking Force. Kakuta was to deliver the attack on Dutch Harbor, on Amaknak Island, then bomb and occupy Adak Island, some 350 kilometres to the west, with a small force of ground troops. At the same time, Hosogaya would be standing by in the heavy cruiser *Nachi* with an invasion force of 2,500 troops between Japan's northern Kurile Islands and the Aleutian islands of Attu and Kiska.

Meanwhile, 1,100 kilometres south, the First Carrier Striking Force of Vice Admiral Chuichi Nagumo steamed toward a decisive confrontation with the American navy at Midway. Admiral Yamamoto directed both operations from his flagship *Yamato* at a point northeast of Midway.

It was June 3, 1942. On the bridge of *Ryujo*, Rear Admiral Kakuta grew impatient with the weather. Clouds hung ominously over the fleet, and radio silence made him unsure of the whereabouts of his other ships, none of which had radar.

The sun would be rising soon in the northern latitude, but at 2:30 A.M., there was no sign of dawn. Outside, the mercury stood at 7°C, and the sea spray froze in slick sheets on the flight decks. Aviation Officer Lieutenant Commander Masatake Okumiya argued against launching an attack under such conditions and advised giving it more time.

Below decks, the aircrews in the ready rooms nervously joked and smoked cigarettes. They had received their latest briefing, their aircraft engines were warmed up with fuel tanks topped, and they could now only wait as apprehension gave way to boredom. Kakuta's warships ploughed on through the ghostly fog to Dutch Harbor. If he was unable to launch his planes and the fog lifted, Kakuta feared enemy aircraft or submarines would surely spot his fleet and thereby jeopardize Yamamoto's entire Midway operation. Bad weather or not, the strike would go ahead, he resolved; the success of Midway depended on his actions.

In the grey inkling of first light, the watch on *Ryujo* reported carrier *Junyo* was 900 metres off the port side. The force was 170 kilometres south of Dutch Harbor. With the fog now lifting, Aviation Officer Okumiya informed the admiral that it would be safe to launch his planes. Kakuta nodded to Lieutenant Commander Okada, who then gave the order to launch the attack. On the decks of the two carriers, pilots climbed into their planes and stood ready, their engines breaking the morning silence with an ever-growing war cry. The signal came at approximately 3 A.M., and one by one the fleet of bombers, dive-bombers and Zeros took off into a cloud ceiling of only 223 metres. In the rolling seas, *Ryujo* went bow first into the trough of a wave just as a bomber was lifting off, throwing it into the sea. The single propeller dug into the water, and the plane started sinking nose first into the frigid water. The two crewmen escaped as the plane disappeared under *Ryujo*'s bow and were spared an icy death by the swift action of an escort destroyer.

The airborne planes circled the two carriers, waiting to group, the glory of the epic aerial attack on Pearl Harbor beckoning the pilots on. Today they would have the honour of delivering the second carrier-launched strike directly against American territory. After the last planes had joined them, the two formations headed north for Dutch Harbor.

Patrolling the waters south of Unalaska, a lone American PBY, a twin-engine flying boat, stumbled into a break in the fog and was immediately pounced upon by pilot Lieutenant Yoshiro Shiga, who was leading a pack of Zeros. Shiga's planes shot it down, killing three of the crew instantly. The remaining five airmen crawled aboard a life raft in the freezing waves, but two more crewmen, including the pilot, died shortly after. The survivors were picked up by the Japanese and gained the dubious distinction of becoming the first American prisoners in the Alaskan war.

Shiga had lost valuable time chasing the American plane. With his air group once again in the fog, he became hopelessly lost and radioed *Junyo* for permission to return to the ship. Alaska's unpredictable weather would not give the Japanese pilots the same easy victory they had enjoyed at Pearl Harbor six months earlier.

The fog also made it impossible for *Ryujo*'s planes to maintain formation, compelling flight leader Lieutenant Masayuki Yamagami to order his planes to find their own way to Dutch Harbor, where they would regroup before the attack. The Japanese aircrews had only outdated maps of Unalaska and Dutch Harbor, copied from old Russian whaling charts. There were many gaps in the drawings where shorelines were unexplored, so that the pilots did not even know the outline of Dutch Harbor from the air. Still, they skillfully managed to locate the target.

The American code-breaking unit "Magic" had correctly reasoned that Dutch Harbor was the likeliest target for a diversionary attack by the Japanese in the north, and anti-aircraft guns, manned 24 hours a day, were in place around the harbour. At 5:40 A.M., the seaplane tender USS *Gillis* signalled the radio tower overlooking Dutch Harbor that a group of unidentified aircraft was heading toward the base. The air-raid siren sounded, sending troops equipped with First World War rifles and helmets running from the barracks of the navy base and Fort Mears army base to the trenches and gun batteries around Dutch Harbor.

The troops had run through the drill many times during practices and false alarms. Allied aircraft movements were not broadcast, so it was common to have a cautionary air-raid alert. As the planes passed over Unalaska's Pyramid Peak and re-formed over Captain's Bay, the soldiers assumed them to be another patrol from nearby Fort Glenn, the secret American base on Umnak Island, and let down their guard. Reconnaissance missions by submarine-launched Japanese planes had not scouted the mainland or islands immediately west of Dutch Harbor, thus American air bases built under the guise of fish canneries at Umnak Island and Cold Bay on the Alaska Peninsula had remained undisclosed to the enemy.

Suddenly a Zero peeled off to strafe the barracks at Fort Mears. Behind, a Kate let loose its bombs on the wooden barracks, killing 25 men. Anti-aircraft batteries on the ground opened fire as two more Zeros swooped down on a lumbering Catalina flying boat that was attempting to take off. Bullets tore into the mail plane, killing two civilian passengers as the seaplane erupted in flames. Tracers strafed two more PBYs moored in the harbour, while one flying-boat crew managed to get airborne. Climbing over Captain's Bay, the PBY came up under a Zero emerging from a run on the base. The waist gunner opened fire at the same time as the machine gunners on the ground, hitting their mark. The Zero burst into flames and plummeted into the harbour as the trundling, ungainly PBY disappeared into the fog, pursued by two Zeros.

In the radio shack overlooking the harbour, the navy signalman could not get a response from Fort Glenn. The wireless telegraph set at the secret base had failed, and the fighter pilots, only 66 kilometres west of the action, were unaware of the attack. The radioman on duty at Cold Bay, 288 kilometres east, picked up the distress signal and sent fighter pilots running for their Curtiss P-40 Warhawks and roaring off to Dutch Harbor.

Back at Dutch Harbor, a Kate light bomber dropped a 225-kilogram (500-pound) bomb on the radio tower, blowing gaping holes around the radio shack and shattering its windows. Rattled but unhurt, the signalman resumed his tapping of the wireless set moments later.

In Anchorage, Juneau and Ketchikan, civilians had been advised to take shelter in the surrounding vast wilderness in the event of an air raid, while Prince Rupert residents had been drilled to whisk children away to the safety of the rainforest. It now appeared the rumours of an impending attack by the Japanese were true. The north was under attack.

After tearing up the village of Dutch Harbor for 20 minutes, the Japanese planes disappeared into the mist over the vast sea. When the fighters from Cold Bay finally roared in some 20 minutes later, the barracks at Fort Mears were in flames and an inky cloud of smoke billowed from a burning army truck below. The enemy was long gone.

As the Japanese pilots withdrew from Dutch Harbor and flew over Makushin Bay, they noted the four old destroyers in the bay and radioed ahead to *Ryujo* for reinforcements. Kakuta ordered *Junyo*'s planes back into the air to find and

American soldiers take cover during the first strike at Dutch Harbor on June 3, 1942. Seventy-five Americans were killed in the two attacks. US DEPT. OF THE ARMY

destroy the American ships. Four Mitsubishi F1M "Pete" float planes were catapulted from *Maya* and *Takao* to act as scouts for *Junyo*'s bombers, but as the weather worsened, the planes again found themselves lost and had to return to their carrier.

In a squall over the North Pacific, *Ryujo*'s planes headed south to rendezvous with their carrier force. The driving rain streamed across the cockpit canopies, and the warm breath of the pilots fogged the inside of the clear shell and made the visibility even worse. Visibility was now down to only 50 metres, as the heavy black clouds forced the planes perilously close to the breaking waves. Salt spray whipped up by the propellers threatened to choke the engines, and the pilots had to break formation to find their own way back to the carriers. Incredibly, all but the plane lost at Dutch Harbor returned safely.

The squall had now passed over Fort Glenn on Umnak Island, and men there could see smoke billowing up from Dutch Harbor. Umnak scrambled 21 P-40s to investigate. Into the clear skies over Umnak stumbled the four Petes launched by the Japanese cruisers. Two Warhawks immediately machine-gunned one Pete, sending it into the water in pieces, while the others headed to the receding storm for cover. The P-40s raked them with machine-gun fire, and a second Pete crashed into the churning sea south of Umnak. The two remaining scout planes somehow managed to elude the fighters and sent frantic calls to the Japanese ships. Badly damaged, they crash-landed next to *Takao* and sank as their riddled pontoons and fuselages filled with water.

Both crews clambered to safety on a boarding net let down over *Takao*'s side. In a debriefing, they described how they'd been jumped by American fighters over Umnak Island. Kakuta concluded that prior air reconnaissance had not been thorough enough—somewhere in the islands was a secret American air base. The Japanese immediately roused the three Americans taken prisoner when the PBY went down. Slapping them about, they demanded to know where the P-40s had suddenly appeared from. Then they brought the captives on deck and threatened to throw them overboard unless they divulged information about a secret fighter base. The prisoners denied knowledge of any such base. Their captors apparently believed their pleas of ignorance, for the Americans were returned to *Takao*'s brig, where they spent three more weeks. They eventually ended up in a Japanese prison camp for the duration of the war.

Before the long day came to a close, American lieutenant J.D. Campbell's PBY stumbled on the Japanese carriers 900 kilometres southwest of Kodiak. Five Zeros flying cover for the force closed in and shot Campbell's plane up so badly he had to ditch it in the roiling sea. The crew escaped and was later picked up by the US Coast Guard cutter *Nemaha*. Concerned that the downed PBY might have radioed his fleet's location, Kakuta ordered a withdrawal to the northwest. Almost as one, the ships turned to port and slipped back into the swirling mass of cloud that had delivered them to North American's shores.

* * *

Admiral Kakuta had successfully carried out the first half of Yamamoto's Alaskan offensive with the attack on Dutch Harbor. His Second Carrier Striking Force now moved to attack a second American target—Adak Island, 880 kilometres to the west. Rear Admiral Sentaro Omori's occupation force of 1,200 troops was sailing east from the

Kuriles to occupy Adak after a pre-invasion bombardment by Kakuta's planes and cruisers and was to quell any
resistance that might exist on the island. To the south, the
First Carrier Striking Force was due to launch its attack on
Midway in a matter of hours.

On the morning of June 4, a wet, grey blanket of cloud
still draped the North Pacific as dawn broke. Rain squalls
occasionally washed across *Ryujo*'s flight deck, cutting visibility to less than 100 metres as fog steamed off the ocean.
In *Ryujo*'s war room, Aviation Officer Masatake Okumiya
told officers and pilots about the Adak operation. Among
them were Admiral Kakuta and his senior staff officer,
Commander Masanori Odagiri. As usual, Okumiya lec-
tured, the weather was bad, and it was deteriorating as
the fleet moved west. The fleet's speed was now reduced
to 10 knots, he added. He told the men that somewhere
in the eastern islands the Americans had successfully
installed a secret fighter base. That alone could thwart
Omori's invasion of Adak and would certainly make the
island difficult to hold once it was taken. The weather over
Dutch Harbor was likely better, as the easterly storms
tended to slow toward the Alaskan coast, and Okumiya
suggested they make a second strike against Dutch Harbor
rather than attacking Adak. The pilots now had a good
idea of Dutch Harbor's layout but knew little of Adak's.
Kakuta gave the order: the invasion of Adak would be
postponed; instead, they would attack Dutch Harbor a

second time. A message was relayed to Admiral Hosogaya and a course change ordered to the northeast.

At noon, a US Navy PBY discovered the Japanese fleet and attacked, only to be shot up by flak bursts. It managed to limp away. Another PBY soon came across the fleet, but a cover of Zeros brought it down with all hands. One by one, American planes found and lost the enemy fleet as it slipped in and out of the Aleutian fog. A lone Martin B-26 Marauder launched an aerial torpedo at *Ryujo* but missed. The bomber returned hastily to Cold Bay to re-arm and refuel, then went back out looking for the fleet. The crew found it but was never heard from again. The wrecked Marauder was discovered some time later on the Alaskan Peninsula; it had apparently crashed after being shot up trying to return to Cold Bay.

By now, every available plane in the area was airborne, searching for the elusive Japanese fleet. When two B-17 Mitchells ran across it and attacked, one was blown out of the sky and the other, wounded, flew back to Cold Bay. Three Marauders also found the Japanese and dropped their torpedoes, but the swells took the missiles off course. For all the dogged attacks by American planes, the Japanese fleet remained unscathed.

Below *Junyo*'s decks, Petty Officer Zenji Abe listened to the commander of flight operations go over his pre-attack briefings. Hailed as the youngest of the Japanese pilots in the attack on Pearl Harbor, Zenji Abe and his brother pilots now received a dressing-down from their superior because only *Ryujo*'s planes had made it to Dutch Harbor in the first strike. The charge must have stung Abe as unfair. After all, a Kate light bomber could bomb in level flight, while the Aichi Val bomber he flew had to pick its target and dive from 3,200 metres. The cloud ceiling over Dutch Harbor had only been a few hundred metres.

Rain pelted the planes on *Ryujo*'s flight deck as they readied for takeoff. The Mitsubishi Zero's propellers drove the water back across their windscreens, rendering it nearly impossible for Flight Petty Officer Tadayoshi Koga to make out the signalman at the end of the flight deck. Koga, a brash young airman with a great dislike for Americans, felt honoured to be chosen as one of the 28 pilots assigned to make the second attack on Dutch Harbor. Koga had been indoctrinated into the military school of thought that revered Japan's pilots as modern-day Samurai. By tradition, he had left clippings of his hair, fingernails and toenails with relatives in Japan so they would have something of him to bury if he should not return from battle. At a sign from the signalman, Koga's Zero roared to the end of *Ryujo*'s deck and lifted off into the black sky to join a force of 27 other Zeros, Kate bombers and Val dive-bombers headed to finish off Dutch Harbor.

At Fort Mears, civilian construction crews were nearing the end of their 12-hour shift on board S.S. *Northwestern*, an old Alaska Steamships vessel appropriated for use as a floating barracks, mess and generation plant. At around

4:30 P.M., two waves of Zeros suddenly swooped down over Unalaska Island, firing as they roared across Dutch Harbor. Bullets tore up the loading dock next to the old steamer as work crews raced for safety. From 3,300 metres above, one pilot put his Val into a screaming dive with *Northwestern* in his crosshairs. Releasing his 225-kilogram (500-pound) bomb, he pulled his plane away from the attack as the old liner exploded into flame amidships. Bombs from the Kates demolished the wooden wharf of the naval air station as Zeros strafed the meagre pickings around the harbour. Bombs killed the four-man crew defending an anti-aircraft battery and all but destroyed the wood-frame hospital in a burst of flying timber and glass. An explosion lit up the village as a rack of bombs ignited 3.4 million litres of fuel stored in wooden tanks. The roar shattered windows all over the island and sent a black mushroom cloud billowing skyward.

The blast could be heard at Umnak, 65 kilometres to the west, and a squadron of P-40 Warhawks, the Aleutian Tigers of the 11th Air Force, scrambled to investigate. In the ensuing dogfight, the Tigers knocked out two Japanese bombers and two Zeros over the cluster of islands, while two of their own planes were shot down. With the sudden appearance of the American fighters, and with their second mission complete, the Japanese attack planes swarmed south for *Ryujo* and *Junyo*. When the smoke cleared over Dutch Harbor, the toll for the Americans was 78 dead and 14 aircraft lost in the two attacks. The Japanese lost 15 airmen and 11 planes.

But the day was not over for the Americans, nor for Tadayoshi Koga. Escorting a Nakajima Kate over tiny Unalga Island, northeast of Unalaska, Koga and five wingmen spotted a lone PBY turning back toward Cold Bay. Flown by Albert E. Mitchell, PBY 42-P-4 had been warned away from the area moments earlier, as the second attack on Dutch Harbor was underway. Immediately the six Zeros swooped down on the lumbering flying boat and opened fire, sending it plummeting toward Unalga Pass below. Even as it went down, the stricken craft's waist gunners continued to fire back, hitting Koga's Zero. Army observers at nearby Brundage Point on Unalaska watched in horror as the survivors of the PBY who had made it into life rafts were all machine-gunned to death by circling Zeros.

Koga's Zero took a bullet through an oil-pressure indicator line, and the overheating engine began to sputter and stall. Koga confidently broadcast an SOS that was picked up by one of the Japanese submarines standing lifeboat duty around Unalaska Island that day. He then glided his plane to Akutan Island, just north of Dutch Harbor, and put his wheels down for what should have been a perfect landing. The landing gear dug deep into the soft Aleutian muskeg, flipped the plane and broke Koga's neck.

The Japanese had come to Dutch Harbor under cover of an enveloping fog and so the fleet retreated. For five weeks following the attacks, Koga's Zero lay undisturbed until spotted by an observant PBY crew. The Alaskan muskeg, so

This Japanese Zero fighter plane piloted by Tadayoshi Koga was found intact five weeks after the attacks on Dutch Harbor. It was the first Zero captured by the Allies and was repaired so engineers could use it as a model for future fighters. US DEPT. OF THE ARMY

troublesome to the military, had won it a valuable prize—the first Mitsubishi Zero captured in the war. Salvaged and sent to the army's aeronautical testing facility in California, the Zero was found to have suffered only minor damage and was soon made airworthy again. Consequently, American pilots and engineers were able to thoroughly study what was then the fastest, longest-range and deadliest of all fighter planes. This was the beginning of the end of Japan's fighter superiority in the Pacific. The Allies could now benefit from the Zero's advanced technology, as well as learn from its shortcomings, and develop new tactics and aircraft that would eventually chase Japan's wonder plane from the Pacific.

CHAPTER

6

Wilderness Warriors: The Alaska Territorial Guard, Pacific Coast Militia Rangers and Fishermen's Volunteer Reserve

THE JAPANESE ATTACKS ON Dutch Harbor were a deadly reminder of what had been obvious for many years—Alaska and the Canadian northwest were not ready to defend against enemy forces. Save for a few coastal squadrons, the whole barren coast in the area of Nome, on Alaska's Seward Peninsula, lay open and virtually undefended with few resources to warn of an enemy attack. As early as the 1930s, Alaskans had urged Congress to approve some form of military presence for Alaska, but these requests were largely ignored. In 1935, Brigadier General Billy Mitchell professed to Congress that "Alaska is the most strategic place in the whole world, the jumping off point to Asia and Japan." Fairbanks, at the centre of Alaska, was within 6,400 kilometres of every important northern capital. Mitchell already viewed Tokyo, which was then staking claims in Manchuria, as the new threat in the Pacific. The Aleutian Islands could provide the stepping stones for an invading army from Asia right to North America, and whoever controlled Alaska could control the world.

Prior to 1940, there was virtually no American military presence in the territory (Alaska would not become a state until 1959), and US defences there consisted of one army outpost, the Chilkoot Barracks, on the Canadian border at Haines. This fort had been built to maintain order during the Klondike Gold Rush and housed a small garrison armed with First World War helmets and rifles. There was no armament larger than a .303 rifle. Only a few hundred soldiers guarded the whole vast Alaska territory.

In 1940, however, Congress decided some form of military expenditure was needed for the northern territory, and it formed the Alaska Defense Command, which would direct all aspects of land, sea and air defence. The task of putting together the newly created force fell to Lieutenant General Simon Bolivar Buckner Jr., a high-achieving West Point graduate from Kentucky, whose father had been a Confederate

Lieutenant General Simon Bolivar Buckner Jr. commanded all Allied forces in Alaska. US DEPT. OF THE ARMY

general in the Civil War. Buckner's ability to skirt formal command protocol to get what he needed was a requisite for survival in the North. He got the go-ahead to construct air bases at Anchorage, Yakutat, Kodiak Island and Annette Island. Naval seaplane bases were also slated for Dutch Harbor, Kodiak and Sitka.

Despite the inception of the Alaska Defense Command, and acutely suspicious of Japanese hostility in the years prior to the attack on Pearl Harbor, Alaska's Governor Ernest Gruening had pushed for the establishment of an Alaskan Territorial Guard since he was first elected to office in 1939. Even when an invasion seemed imminent in 1942, Gruening maintained the United States was unable or unwilling to mount an adequate defence of Alaska. Before the Pearl Harbor attack, some military circles had argued that if Japan launched an invasion through the Arctic, Alaska would be impossible to defend and should be abandoned to the enemy. On Kodiak Island, as well as in coastal villages, civilians were issued First World War–vintage rifles with 20 rounds of ammunition each and told they could either surrender to the Japanese or hide out and fight until help arrived. This incensed Gruening, and he pressed Congress for funds to set up militia units in Alaska. His plan was to form Alaskans—trappers, homesteaders, prospectors and, most significant, Native volunteers—into a first line of defence of soldiers and scouts. (The four Arctic Aboriginal groups in Alaska are the Inupiat, Central Alaskan Yu'pik, Alutiiq and Siberian Yupik, but at the time all were speciously referred to as "Eskimo.")

Eskimo soldiers, Gruening argued, were accustomed to surviving and working in a land that offered little sustenance; they would surrender no comfort fighting a guerrilla war against an invader. They also had an intricate knowledge of their home terrain, where no navigable landmarks existed, and were master dog handlers and expert sailors. As to their deftness with a rifle, Gruening wrote, "Had the (enemy) parachutists come, or would they come tomorrow, the deadly accuracy of these Eskimo marksmen would bring them down."

Alaska Territorial Guard

Congress, after much rallying by Gruening and Alaska Representative Anthony Dimond, was persuaded to expend funds for the security of Alaska by signing Bill 122 authorizing the formation of the Alaska Territorial Guard (ATG) in March 1941. Initially, Gruening was allotted enough funding and rifles to outfit two units totalling about 400 men, but after Hawaii was attacked, no limitation was put on the number of recruits. It is estimated that around 20,000 Alaskans joined the ATG, 27 of them women, although the official roster put the number at 6,389. One woman, Laura Beltz Wright, was reputed to be the best sharpshooter in her company. The army assigned Captain Carl Scheibner as an aide to the governor and made him responsible for recruitment in eastern Alaska, while Major Marvin Marston oversaw Alaska's more significant coastal and western region. Marston had served in the American army in the First World War and already had much bush experience working as a prospector in northern Quebec and Ontario. He re-enlisted in the army after precious metals mining was shut down when Canada went to war in 1939. Marston's ability to irritate the upper brass with schemes to store aircraft underground and other eccentric projects made him a prime candidate for posting to Alaska, and he readily accepted the job.

While many considered Alaska a punishment detail, Marston relished the opportunity to be back working in the wild country. Buckner had no time for his type, however, and described Marston as "no damn good," giving him the task of helping the governor recruit the Eskimo. Governor Gruening took an immediate liking to the major and respected his empathy for the Native people. Marston's work had regularly brought him among indigenous people before, and rather than impose white ways on them, he learned their ways of the bush.

Gruening found, on the other hand, that the army in general was bigoted. This was evident in the substandard treatment of black construction battalions sent north, while throughout Alaska the Aboriginals were treated as second-class citizens and segregated from white society. Eskimo people could not sit in the white section of the movie house in Nome, and Native women were prohibited from performing with the United Services Overseas (USO) entertainment troupes in Alaska.

The worst manifestations of this attitude came when the US military uprooted 881 Aleuts from nine villages on the Aleutians and Pribilofs and sent them to five camps in southeastern Alaska, where they were virtually abandoned. They were evacuated with only 24 hours' notice, allowed to take only one suitcase each and forced to leave behind personal items, cultural and religious icons, rifles, boats and dogs. Some were even ordered to torch their villages. At Nazan Bay on Atka, the Aleuts had not even left the village before American soldiers began looting their homes for souvenirs. The internment camps they were moved to were leaking, drafty old canneries and mining camps with no plumbing or electricity. In one camp, 200 residents shared one open toilet located on the seashore. Few of them had even seen a tree before, and now they found themselves corralled in the dense rainforest of southeast Alaska. The treatment the relocated Aleuts received at the hands of their own country was no better than that received by captured Aleuts sent to labour camps in Japan. Over 10 percent of all Aleuts sent to southeast Alaska died during the two to three years of internment.

Despite these affronts, Aleuts and other Aboriginal Alaskans remained resolutely loyal to America. Marston's recruiting efforts took him to the remote villages of the Alaskan Arctic and the islands that lay off the Seward Peninsula. Using aircraft and boats when conditions permitted, he most often made the trek by dog team with the help of an Eskimo guide. Marston found the Aleuts and Eskimos eager to sign up.

Gruening used the recruiting drive to inform the Eskimo of their rights as citizens—most of them did not even know they were Americans—while Marston and Scheibner encouraged them to vote and even run for office. Throughout the campaign, no Eskimo recruits asked to be paid and none turned down the American government's request for help. Boys as young as 12 and men as old as 80, as well as women, enlisted, and all of them were as good with a rifle as the average GI recruit—or better. This eagerness to sign up was mirrored in Canada's North. Many Canadian Aboriginal people saw it as their patriotic duty to enlist in a war that was happening worlds apart from their own remote communities. Some put their traditional skills, honed for survival in the Canadian wilderness, to good use in the army as scouts, observers, sharpshooters and snipers. When asked how he came to be so accurate with a rifle, one Canadian Native undergoing training in the army remarked, "When your dinner is running away from you on four legs, you get to be a good shot."

One of Marston's first challenges was to recruit the Natives on St. Lawrence Island, which lay north of the Aleutians in the Bering Sea, just 160 kilometres east of the Siberian mainland. Few Europeans and other outsiders had travelled there, except for Russian traders early in the century. When Marston made his first trip to the island village of Gambell, he found about 50 Natives and one white man, Frank Daugherty, the Bureau of Indian Affairs schoolteacher. Daugherty's compatriots had abandoned the island, fearing—with good reason—that Alaska would be the next target after Pearl Harbor. In November 1941, before war was declared, a large Japanese warship had appeared off the island and remained for 10 days. During that time, the ship took soundings and troops came ashore, questioning the Natives about the number of reindeer on the island, the inventory of rifles, water sources and other details. Believing this to be part of a larger invasion force, Daugherty hid out and filmed the goings-on with his 8-millimetre camera. The ship then departed east toward mainland Alaska but returned after many days to retrieve a shore party left on the island. The residents had observed their signal fires and later found the remains of the Japanese camp. News of the reconnaissance visit to St. Lawrence was further evidence to Gruening and Buckner that a Japanese invasion was to come from the north.

By 1943, Marston's ATG stood at 20,000 strong, including 3,000 Eskimos who were united for the first time in their history under a single leader into an organized militia. This did not sit well with much of the white population of Alaska, and the US Army began to question Marston's motives, charging him with inciting armed insurrection among Eskimos seeking to secede from the United States. An investigation was launched whereby the Eskimo units' strong loyalty to Marston was scrutinized. Nearly every Native male in the ATG was interrogated and one so severely that he committed suicide in shame after being released.

Marston saw the investigation as an attempt to remove him from Alaska and allow certain military personnel to impose their control over the Natives. Governor Gruening was powerless to interfere with the army's investigation, but after one month of questioning, all charges against Marston and his men were dropped. Still, the incident left many of the Eskimo soldiers too disheartened to return to service.

While the ATG never saw military action, it performed invaluable tasks by serving as the army's eyes and ears on the northern frontier and easing the strain on already-stretched military resources in that area. Later in the war, the ATG's Eskimo units were responsible for the rescue of an air-force crew lost in the Arctic and the downing and recovery of Japanese balloon bombs—noble actions for the humble army of the tundra.

Pacific Coast Militia Rangers

In 1942, a local militia, the Pacific Coast Militia Rangers (PCMR) was formed to protect British Columbia against the real threat of the Japanese and to calm British Columbians after the bombing of Pearl Harbor. Made up of loggers, trappers, ranchers and prospectors who knew the province's terrain well, the PCMR scouted for the army and protected transportation and communication infrastructure. Age was not a factor in enlisting; the militia accepted boys as young as 15 who had proved they could handle a rifle, as well as men too old for regular service. In August 1942, the militia became a corps of the Canadian Army.

Hundreds of men were eager to join this new militia, and soon the number grew to the thousands. Many enlisted because they felt stigmatized as being weak or cowardly for not joining the regular army, despite being needed at home to provide food and maintain wartime industries. At the peak enrolment, there were 15,000 men in the PCMR.

The PCMR had no official military-style uniform, but used water-repellant or Drybak plaid wool pants and jackets. Members also had an armband with the initials PCMR, company number and the local designation. They wore a shooting-style hat with a PCMR hat badge in the centre. If he so desired, a Ranger could use the badge to pin up the left side of the hat, in an Australian style. Rank insignia similar to the regular army were used.

Ranger training sessions were held in highly populated areas, but men who couldn't attend these sessions had the information passed on by other militia members. Soon after the corps' inception, a training publication, *The Ranger*, was begun. It passed on vital information, including articles titled "Know Where to Shoot," "What You Can Do With a Tarp" and "Dig or Die." One issue contained an article celebrating the 50th anniversary of the Winchester Model 1984 .30-30 lever-action rifle. This was the rifle issued to each Ranger. The article stated, "If it killed a bear cleanly for you in the piping times of peace, you can be quite sure it will drill a Jap or any other unwholesome vermin who make the mistake of cluttering up our coast." This rifle was a suitable choice of weapon, as most men were familiar with it in their civilian life and it didn't take crucial munitions away from the regular army, which used No. 4 Lee-Enfield rifles.

After Japan's surrender, the PCMR were disbanded but were re-formed as the Canadian Rangers, or Canadian Rangers Patrol Group. This militia still exists today with

4,700 members, many of them Natives, and they are now issued a No. 4 Lee-Enfield rifle and 200 rounds of ammunition each year. The Rangers are highly identifiable by their bright red sweatshirts, ball caps and safety vests as they carry out their mission "to provide lightly equipped, self-sufficient mobile forces in support of the Canadian Forces sovereignty and domestic operations in Canada."

Fishermen's Volunteer Reserve

Before the outbreak of war, the Canadian government was concerned about the Japanese population on the West Coast. An edict from Japan decreed all males descended from Japanese ancestry were automatically considered reservists of the Japanese navy or army, even those living abroad. The Dominion government was aware that Japanese-Canadian fishermen were very knowledgeable of British Columbia's intricate coastline and that Japanese males, on reaching their 16th birthday, would go to Japan for a year of schooling. These factors served to arouse mistrust toward the Japanese community and called their loyalty into question, even though this was largely unjustified. Added to these suspicions was the problem of defending the coast in case of an actual attack. Since the navy was largely occupied in the Atlantic, a separate force was required to relieve some of the regular navy's patrol duties.

In the summer of 1937, Mr. Roland Bourke, a civilian employee of the naval service, was charged with consulting with fishermen and, if there was enough interest, recruiting them into the Fishermen's Volunteer Reserve (FVR). Fishermen welcomed the idea, and soon Bourke had enough volunteers to proceed.

Fishermen already possessed a good knowledge of the bays and coves where they worked, and they had excellent seamanship skills. As fishermen were involved in food production, a vital war industry, they did not have to sign up for overseas service. The formation of the FVR would solve several problems for the government. The fishermen would continue to provide food for the war effort and their boats could serve as patrol vessels for the resource-strapped navy.

In 1938, Lieutenant Commander Colin Donald, a retired Royal Navy officer living in BC, was commissioned by the Royal Canadian Navy (RCN) to organize the volunteer unit. He was given use of the tug *Skidegate* and travelled up and down the coast, signing up new recruits. The commander no doubt experienced some culture shock going from the starched halls of the Royal Navy to dealing with gruff fishermen on the remote BC coast, but Donald was easygoing and well-liked by the recruits, although he endured some good-natured ribbing along the way.

The fishermen were an eager but somewhat rebellious addition to the navy, as fishing was a solitary profession. They had their own version of regulation dress consisting of a British "pusser" uniform with a trademark Cowichan Indian sweater over it, and gumboots. Some had been liquor smugglers during prohibition or had a strong aversion to mandatory military service. With this in mind the fishermen gained two important concessions for their "Gumboot Navy." They would not be used in industrial disputes, nor would they be used in the regular navy. The seasoned fishermen gave professional advice and opinions, requested or not, to some of the navy's "prairie sailors." This attitude did little to endear them to the regular navy officers.

Before the war, the fishermen trained in seamanship, signalling and patrolling for one month at the Navy base at Esquimalt, near Victoria. Fishboat crews travelled to Esquimalt during the fishing off-season, between late October and April. Some of the FVR vessels were purchased outright by the navy, but a great many were fishboats confiscated from the Japanese-Canadian fishermen who lived along the coast. These served as gate vessels (guard vessels at the entrance to a harbour), ran supplies and performed police and surveillance duties at some of the more remote stations. Once Canada was at war, gunnery and enemy vessel and aircraft identification were added to the FVR training regime.

In July 1942, off the Queen Charlotte Islands, an FVR vessel encountered what the crew assumed was an odd, round buoy that had come loose from its mooring. The crew machine-gunned it until it sank out of harm's way. When they reported its description, they learned it was a Japanese horned-type anti-ship mine—a calling card perhaps left by a prowling enemy submarine. Mines began to turn up with more frequency off the north coast, carried on seasonal currents from

Asia or the Aleutians. One of the deadly devices was recovered in 1972, washed up on the west coast of the Queen Charlottes. Because of this added danger, FVR reservists were paid an extra 25 cents a day when working in the area. The FVR had over 400 vessels, so keeping tabs on them could have been difficult. Due to shortages and imposed radio silence, it was not feasible to supply them all with radios. In response, the FVR came up with the idea of using carrier pigeons on most boats, so navy headquarters could keep track of their whereabouts. Ingenious in its simplicity, the system was nearly impossible to intercept; the pigeons could travel over long distances without relay stations and required little maintenance except daily feeding. The birds, with coded messages attached, could be released from any point on the coast to relay a ship's status and maintain the link between ship and base.

In spite of the FVR's protocol shortcomings, there was no denying their professionalism as sailors. The FVR ships were the only vessels to patrol from Cape Flattery to Alaska in all weather, 24 hours a day, 7 days a week. By doing this, the FVR freed the navy from routine patrol so it could handle the more urgent matters of escort and anti-submarine patrol. The last members of the FVR were discharged by January 1945 once the threat of enemy actions in the Pacific Northwest had subsided.

7

A Road to Victory: The Alaska Highway

BOTH THE CANADIANS AND AMERICANS had long considered building a road connecting the wild northern territories with southern civilization and the lower 48 states, but competing national and regional interests had stalled any progress on the project. Pearl Harbor, and an intercepted Japanese transmission indicating that Alaska would be the likely target of an invasion force, changed everything. In early 1942, it was no longer a matter of when to build a road to Alaska, but how long it would take to build it. Highway access to the North would allow troops to defend North America's northern perimeter against invasion by Japan via Alaska, or possibly by Germany through Siberia, if the Russian front fell. At its narrowest, the Bering Strait separating Siberia and

Alaska is less than 64 kilometres wide. In deep winter it sometimes freezes, narrowing the gap even further for an invading army—literally putting it at North America's back door. An Alaska highway could also be used to ferry much-needed equipment to beleaguered Soviet troops. Also, a road through Canada's North would make it easier to send large numbers of troops to Alaska, where they could use the Aleutian Islands as stepping stones to the Kuriles for an invasion of Japan.

In 1905, the North West Mounted Police, now the Royal Canadian Mounted Police (RCMP), had blazed a trail nearly 640 kilometres long from Fort St. John, BC, toward the Klondike before the end of the gold rush cut short the project at the Stikine River. In the 1930s, BC's pro-western premier Duff Pattullo hounded the federal government to fund a highway to Alaska to help open up northern BC for development. But the Canadian government was not anxious to pour money into a road that it felt would mostly benefit the United States. When Pattullo's attempts to initiate a northern highway project met the immoveable force of Prime Minister Mackenzie King, he turned to the Americans, finding a sympathetic listener in President Franklin Roosevelt. While many Americans supported a road through Canada as the only way to connect Alaska with the continental United States, many in Congress opposed the idea. They, in turn, did not want to pay for a road that they believed would mostly benefit Canadians.

The Canadian government admonished Pattullo for his overtures south of the border on the grounds that such an American-funded highway would threaten the Dominion's security and sovereignty. Out of respect for its northern neighbour, the United States did not push the issue. Pattullo wanted his highway, however, and stoked the fire of western discontent by pointing out that projects in the east were given priority over those in the west, particularly in British Columbia. Pattullo again pressed the Americans, proposing that private entrepreneurs cover the cost of road construction. Again the federal government scolded the upstart premier and refused to consider a road through Canada's North funded by US dollars. Plainly Ottawa did not want a large American presence or investment in its northern territory—that is, until the Japanese threat clearly made this problem the lesser of two evils.

In January 1942, the American and Canadian members of the Pacific Joint Board on Defense recommended that a highway be constructed linking Alaska to the continental United States. By February, the American Cabinet War Committee concurred and approved initial funds and the survey for the new highway's route, even though the US had not been given, nor even requested, Canadian approval for a road that would pass over 1,900 kilometres of Canadian territory.

If the Canadian government had been reluctant to build a northern highway before 1941, the threat of an invasion by Japan via the North Pacific finally prompted Ottawa to change its mind, but with a sobering warning: "The highway goes both ways, to be used by us . . . or an invading army."

When the bill was tabled in Parliament, Ottawa was quick to give agreement and perhaps was even glad to have the Alaska Highway annoyance finally resolved. The Americans would shoulder the greatest portion of the cost and problems associated with a construction project of such magnitude in the unforgiving North. Canada agreed to waive all import duties and taxes on equipment and personnel, provide the right of way through Canadian territory and allow the use of timber, gravel and waterways required for construction. The United States would assume the cost of construction and maintenance up to a period of six months after the war's end, at which point the Canadian section of the highway would be turned over to Ottawa. The US Army Corps of Engineers would be responsible for the initial survey and cutting out a rough road, while the US Public Roads Administration would take responsibility for straightening and grooming the pioneer road.

Three routes had been proposed, but the Dawson Creek through Whitehorse to Fairbanks route was chosen over a shorter coastal route because it would parallel the Northwest Staging Route, an existing series of rough airfields extending from Edmonton, Alberta, to Whitehorse in Yukon. The weather inland was much more stable than that on the coast and, significantly, a coastal highway would be vulnerable to enemy attack from the sea and carrier- or submarine-launched aircraft.

By mid-March 1942, members of the US Army Corps of Engineers had descended on Fort St. John to begin survey work for what was dubbed "the Highway to Tokyo." The new road would have its southern terminus at Dawson Creek and end 2,470 kilometres away at Fairbanks, Alaska. Much of the groundwork on the first leg of the Alaska Highway was already done for the American army engineers. Knox McCusker of the Dominion Land Survey of Canada had completed surveying and mapping a route in the north Peace River district and had roughed out a 75-kilometre road between Dawson Creek and Fort St. John. As well, the Dominion Land Survey had come up with a method of road surveying using an aircraft as a sighting platform. The Canadian engineers who devised this method were brought on board and were responsible for much of the initial routing work on the Alaska Highway.

Seven US Army construction battalions did the initial road clearing through the wilderness. Three of them were entirely composed of black enlisted men from the American south. They were commanded by white officers, as it was assumed in the US Army at the time that black men were only fit for support duty. The black soldiers were given no opportunity to acclimatize to the harsh northern weather and the relentless building schedule, and many found the conditions devastating. There were significantly more suicides among the black soldiers than among their white compatriots.

A Road to Victory

Road construction was maintained for 22 hours a day to meet the rigorous deadline, much of this during the winter when temperatures remained well below zero. When the temperature fell to -50°C, the stocks of antifreeze for heavy machinery froze solid. Motors were left running and smudge pots were positioned under the engines to keep them from freezing. Truck drivers were at first told that if they ditched a truck, it was five days of kitchen police duty (KP). As the kitchens were located in warm buildings and driving trucks was a bitterly cold duty, there were soon more soldiers on KP than driving trucks. The "punishment" was soon rescinded.

The soldiers' tents were heated by wood that was cut by hand since the chain saws of that time were large and unwieldy and had to be operated by two men. This meant that wood cutting was a constant occupation, as illustrated by the following anecdote. While trying to estimate how much wood was needed to get through the winter, one army officer decided to consult an elderly and wise-looking Native. The Native told him it was going to be a bad winter and very cold. When the officer asked how he knew this, the man just repeated his response. When the officer again pressed the Native for a reason for his prediction, asking him what signs he saw to foresee a cold winter, the Native simply answered, "See many white men cutting much wood . . . be very bad winter."

In the summer, men worked in the waist-deep, sucking

muskeg in relentless swarms of blackflies and hordes of mosquitoes "as big as Zeros." There were also predatory bears and cougars, and the rugged country posed other dangers. Seven men were killed when their log raft overturned as they shot the rapids of a river; others died as vehicles and earthmoving equipment slid down embankments and overturned on the soft muskeg.

As noted above, the road roughly followed the path of the Northwest Staging Route, a string of primitive airfields hewn out of the wilderness by the Canadian government in the 1920s to service remote areas of northern Alberta through BC to the Yukon Territory. It was intended to join up with a string of American airfields planned for Alaska through the Aleutians and on to the Orient to form the much-touted Great Circle Route. By the time war came, the Americans had instituted an urgent program to develop airfields in Alaska for military defence.

While the route was used to rush men, supplies, equipment and aircraft to vulnerable sectors for use against Japan in the expected attacks on Alaska, it served a much larger role in the Second World War. Over 8,000 aircraft were moved north along the route to Nome as part of the Alaska to Siberia Lend-Lease program to the Soviet Union. In Nome and Fairbanks, Soviet pilots took possession of aircraft and flew them across the Bering Strait to Siberia and on to the Russian front in the desperate struggle for survival against Germany. Once the air route was fully established, it was no more unusual to see Bell P39 Aircobras and Dakota DC-3s with the red star of the Soviet Air Force passing north through Montana, Edmonton and BC than it was to see planes with the American star or the RCAF roundel. At Nome, there were as many Soviet officers as American in town, desperately stocking up in the small stores and shops before heading home to war-starved Russia.

As more men and equipment moved north, lack of a reliable supply of petroleum threatened to grind the war effort to a halt. Alaska needed petroleum imported in significant quantity by tanker ships from the south, but neither the United States nor Canada could provide enough tankers and the warships or planes to escort them along the Pacific coast. If the Allies were to eventually launch an invasion of Japan via Alaska and the Aleutians, they would need a steady, protected and preferably local supply of oil in the North.

The Americans turned their attention to Norman Wells in the Northwest Territories, where huge reserves had been discovered in 1920. There was a small refinery there, but it only produced enough to supply local needs. Pumping stations, pipelines and a larger refining capacity were needed to maintain the defence of Alaska and the Canadian North. The United States requested and received permission from the Canadian government to develop the fields as well as to construct a refinery at Whitehorse, some 800 kilometres south. In May 1942, a complete, operational refinery in Texas was dismantled and shipped north via Prince Rupert and Skagway, then reassembled at Whitehorse. At the same time, the pipeline and the Canol Road (an access road from Norman Wells on the Mackenzie River to Whitehorse) were built by the US Army Corps of Engineers and a consortium of companies later to become BPC (Betchel, Price, Callaghan), which was headquartered in San Francisco. It took 20 months to build 2,897 kilometres of pipeline and 3,219 kilometres of road, and workers on both projects encountered the same challenges as had been faced during the construction of the Alaska Highway. The following flyer was posted for prospective employees at an employment office:

June 15 42
THIS IS NO PICNIC

Working and living conditions on this job are as difficult as those encountered on any construction job ever done in the United States or foreign territory. Men hired for this job will be required to work and live under the most extreme conditions imaginable. Temperature will range from 90 degrees above zero to 70 degrees below zero. Men will have to fight swamps, rivers, ice and cold. Mosquitos, flies and gnats will not only be annoying but will cause bodily harm. If you are not prepared to work under these and similar conditions

Do Not Apply

Bechtel-Price-Callahan

Despite all difficulties, oil production began in April 1944; however, the refinery operated for only a year before being shut down in April 1945. Many construction sites along the Canol pipeline highway have never been cleaned up, as most of the camps are very isolated. Many artifacts, such as army trucks and road-building equipment, still lie there rusting. Today the Canol Road is accessible for vehicles to the Yukon/Northwest Territory border; at that point it becomes the Canol Heritage Trail.

Detractors in the US Senate later launched an investigation into Canol, claiming the project had been conducted secretly and ended as a $100-million waste of American war dollars. Furthermore, they said, the money had been spent developing a Canadian oil project with no negotiation of post-war rights for the United States. Canol, however, produced over a million barrels of oil for the war effort and would have been invaluable had the Allies chosen to invade Japan by way of Alaska.

Northern megaprojects like the Alaska Highway and Northwest Staging Route gave local Native people seasonal work in traditional roles as suppliers of game and firewood or as casual labourers. But the invading armies of construction crews also brought the ills of "civilization" north with them, which profoundly affected Native society. While hospitals in Fort St. John and Whitehorse were expanded to the benefit of the Natives, diseases brought by outsiders boosted their need for such facilities. Epidemics of mumps, measles, influenza, meningitis, whooping cough, dysentery, diphtheria and tuberculosis ran rampant through Native populations living close to the new highway. Mortality among Native infants peaked at 47 percent in 1943–44, triple its pre-war rate. Among a test group of Natives living near the highway, 49 percent were infected with tuberculosis, while others living in outlying areas were unaffected by the new maladies.

In the frontier setting of highway towns, alcohol passed freely from road crew to Native as a means of bridging the cultural gap. Outsiders entered into short-term relationships with Native women, resulting in an explosion in the number of illegitimate children, who were then abandoned by their fathers when the crews returned south or moved on. In a span of less than one year, as the Alaska Highway was bulldozed through their traditional territory, the lives of Yukon Natives were dramatically and forever changed by a war thousands of kilometres away.

In Whitehorse, the population swelled from about 400 to over 7,000 inhabitants within a year, while Dawson Creek boomed from 400 to 4,000 people almost overnight. A tent city was erected at Dawson Creek, and necessities like water and firewood were trucked in to support this instant town. The number of American personnel, both army and civilian, in Canada's North eventually numbered nearly 50,000, and they were cordially referred to by northerners as the "army of occupation."

A Road to Victory

The huge American troop presence in Canada's North did not go unnoticed, nor was it taken lightly. The British High Commissioner to Canada, Malcolm Macdonald, pointed out to the Canadian government the seriousness of having such a large foreign presence in its north. Macdonald was suspicious of American motives for constructing such megaprojects as the Alaska Highway, Canol and the development in the Canadian North and was concerned about the lack of involvement by Canadians themselves. If the Americans decided to claim sovereignty and stay put once the war was over, Canada would be able to do little about it.

Prime Minister William Lyon Mackenzie King decided that a Canadian authority should be in place to protect the interests of Canada and appointed Major General W.W. Foster to oversee American activities in the North. The matter of US involvement came to a head when Imperial Oil denied Foster access to information, saying that it first had to clear access through United States authorities. Foster applied for the information again and was refused, this time on grounds of national security. The matter went to the highest levels of the two governments before Foster's authority was established.

While Macdonald was right to question the integrity of American intentions in the North, he also made suggestions that put the matter to rest. Canadians needed more participation in their own northern territory on these megaprojects, their government deemed, and for this they paid the Americans nearly $124 million—a phenomenal sum to be diverting from the war acquisition budget. It gave Canadians control of their section of the Alaska Highway and won permanent improvements to the Northwest Staging Route from the Americans, who in effect became contractors to the Canadian government. Ultimately, this expensive but prudent manoeuvre removed any question of Canadian dominion in the North.

Even by today's standards, the Alaska Highway is an amazing feat of modern engineering. It was officially opened on November 20, 1942, above Kluane Lake, Yukon, at a spot respectfully named Soldier's Summit. Winding 2,228 kilometres from Dawson Creek to Fairbanks, the road was officially opened for public use in 1946. Originally, a permit was required to travel on this gravel, tire-shredding road, but over time it has been upgraded to an almost fully paved highway.

8

The RCAF in Alaska

IN THE MONTHS FOLLOWING THE attack on Pearl Harbor on December 7, 1941, the United States began to move soldiers, ships and, most important, squadrons into undefended Alaska. American code breakers were able to decrypt most of the Japanese navy codes and to decipher from Japanese transmissions that an attack was planned on Alaska, likely at Dutch Harbor in the eastern Aleutians. Still, Alaska was of low priority and the Americans had few squadrons to expend on the territory. As a result, the US requested that Canada send squadrons there.

Based at Patricia Bay near Victoria, BC, RCAF No. 115 Bomber-Reconnaissance Squadron, flying twin-engine Bristol Bolingbrokes, was transferred to cover the sea approaches to Prince Rupert and southeast Alaska. By May 10, 1942, the first ground crew and a Canadian army unit arrived and set up camp on Annette Island, Alaska, 121 kilometres north of Prince Rupert. The only residents of Annette lived at Metlakatla, a Native village six kilometres from the base, and some US Army personnel. Upon arrival, the Canadians found few permanent structures had been erected, so they were forced to live in tents. Latrine, bathing and laundry facilities were non-existent and the incessant rain had turned the dirt runways to mud. The night they arrived was made all the more memorable when the ammunition dump caught fire—presumably started by an aircraft landing flare—and erupted in explosions and bullet shots. Fired by the rumours of invasion, all took cover and laid low until they were confident that Japanese troops were not invading the island.

Another Canadian squadron followed No. 115 to Annette Island in June 1942. Already partway across the country from Dartmouth, Nova Scotia, to their new base at Patricia Bay, the No. 118 Fighter Squadron, flying Kittyhawks (the Canadian version of the P-40), was diverted to Annette Island. No. 118 had extensive anti-submarine experience in the Atlantic hunting German U-boats, and some of the pilots were already battle-hardened veterans. Squadron Leader Arthur Yuile had flown in the Battle of Britain and had several kills to his credit. He had been shot down once, shot up once and wounded once. At the height of the air blitz over England, Yuile had flown three gruelling sorties in seven hours, fighting off German bombers, for which he received the Distinguished Flying Cross.

No. 118's new duties were to reinforce No. 115 and provide fighter support for Prince Rupert. After an arduous five-day transcontinental flight from their base in Dartmouth, 15 P-40 Kittyhawks and two Hudson aircraft landed at Annette Island. This was believed to be the longest overland flight ever undertaken by a fighter group, and two P-40s were lost after they had to make forced landings.

Life quickly fell into a monotonous routine on Annette Island. Initially there were no aircraft hangars, so ground crews worked in unheated tents draped over the planes' engines, performing maintenance in highly disagreeable weather. Besides the pressures of maintaining combat-ready squadrons, artillery and infantry units, the personnel had to cope with primitive conditions reminiscent of those endured by early settlers. The base lacked running water, electricity, bunks and barracks. Men had to thaw water when the temperature dipped below freezing and keep a steady supply of firewood chopped for the wood stoves. The unpaved runway was full of rocks, roots and potholes, and the constant rain caused aircraft to sink into the field up to their landing wheels. Endless boredom, bad weather and the austere conditions had many men requesting a return to overseas assignments.

Despite their reclusive posting, the squadrons did manage some limited action. While on anti-submarine patrol, RCAF Bomber 9118 of the No. 115 attacked a purported submarine 130 kilometres northwest of Annette Island on July 9. The US Coast Guard cutter *McLane*, patrol boat *YP-251* and HMCS *Quatsino* converged on the location, where *McLane* picked up a sound contact. Over the course of the day, *McLane* laid down several depth-charge patterns. Reportedly, a torpedo was fired from the submarine and passed under *YP-251*. After *McLane* responded by depth-charging the area, large air bubbles, oil and a material resembling rock wool that was used as an insulator boiled to the surface. Following the war, the Japanese navy reported no submarines lost in that area. Whatever happened in this incident, the crew of RCAF Bomber 9118 and US Coast Guard cutter *McLane* received commendations for their aggressive response in the "Battle of Annette Island."

The No. 115 Squadron's arrival in Alaska wrote two minor footnotes in American military history. Canada became the first and only allied foreign power to set up a military base on United States soil and the only foreign nation to directly assume defence of American territory.

The war had proceeded agreeably for the men of RCAF No. 8 Bomber-Reconnaissance Squadron, another Bolingbroke unit. Flying anti-submarine duty out of Sea Island near Vancouver, they enjoyed weekend dances with plenty of female company at the Palomar and Cave dance halls and were sometimes treated to dinner with local families. Plenty of American liquor and cigarettes could be picked up cheaply on refuelling stops at McChord and Whidby air stations in neighbouring Washington State. As Harry Bray, a pilot with No. 8, reminisced, "War wasn't exactly hell."

These amenities came to an abrupt end when No. 8's commanding officer informed the men that because a Japanese invasion force might strike at Alaska at any moment, the squadron was being sent north to help out the US Army Air Forces (USAAF). The squadron was to proceed north as soon as possible. Their Bristol Bolingbrokes were fitted with new American .50-calibre turrets on the fuselage, and after a stop at Paine Field in Washington to be refitted for American bombs, 12 bombers of No. 8 Squadron headed north on June 2.

The trip north took the squadron through some of the most isolated airstrips on the continent. The aircraft made refuelling stops at Port Hardy, Bella Bella, Terrace and Annette Island before continuing north to Juneau and then Yakutat. At each town where No. 8's bombers set down along the way, the Alaskans treated the Canadian aircrew like liberating heroes. Nothing was too good to lavish on the RCAF, and the Alaskans showed their appreciation by giving the Canadians free drinks, dinners and souvenirs. When the squadron continued north, one Juneau business owner had to sheepishly request the return of the deed to his store. Apparently, even Alaska's renowned generosity knew some limits.

In the days following the attacks, Alaska remained on high alert. As the 12 bombers of No. 8 touched down at Yakutat, reports of submarine sightings were coming in, and lurking somewhere in the fog was a force of Japanese warships poised to strike. The planes were ordered to depart immediately for Anchorage, where the enemy might strike next. The Bolingbrokes' exhausted crews immediately refuelled and headed out. With radio silence now in effect across Alaska and with sketchy charts and minimal visibility, they made their way by dead reckoning across the tip of the Kenai Peninsula. (A risky method of navigation, dead reckoning involves taking one's last known position and calculating one's current position and the time to reach the destination by estimating speed, taking into account wind and other factors.) The planes stayed just above the waves before circling over the Kenai Glacier and dropping into Anchorage.

Before landing in Anchorage, however, the radio operator of the lead Bolingbroke received an SOS from one of his planes that was lost and low on fuel. He lost contact when his own low-flying plane's trailing antenna was knocked off by a trestle bridge. Still, the stray Bolingbroke persisted. It had pulled into a steep climb to avoid crashing into the wall of a rock face or glacier, but when it came up into the sunshine, its crew had no idea where they were. Radio contact was vital if they were to get down through the jagged peaks of the Kenai, so Flying Officer Pappy Deeks took a chance and broke radio silence. After several desperate calls to the radio range at Cordova south of Anchorage received no reply, he radioed, "I know you are down there. We need that range. If you don't turn it on and we survive, you damn well won't!" The radio range abruptly came back on the air, allowing Deeks and his crew a safe passage to Anchorage.

At the time of No. 8's dispatch to Alaska, the RCAF also sent north No. 111 Fighter Squadron, flying Kittyhawks, to be based at Anchorage. Eventually, a component of the squadron was to take up station on Umnak Island, 145 kilometres west of Dutch Harbor. The seven Kittyhawks were making their way down the Alaska Peninsula when the weather turned foul. Two planes were damaged in landing at Cold Bay, and the squadron had to wait several days for replacement aircraft. At the southern tip of the Bering Sea, Umnak was still another 320 kilometres west across frigid, storm-tossed waters. The Canadians took off on July 16, but the weather continued to play havoc. With less than 64 kilometres left to go, they hit a wall of infamous Aleutian fog over Dutch Harbor. As the planes executed a turn to return to Cold Bay, the pilots lost visual contact and four Kittyhawks slammed into Unalaska Island while a fifth crashed into the sea. Among the fatalities was Squadron Leader J.W. Kerwin, a battle-seasoned pilot on rotation from Europe. Frantic radio calls from Dutch Harbor to the missing fighters were met only by an eerie static. Within the span of a few days, the weather had claimed seven of the squadron's Kittyhawks—half of its fighter strength, before any of the fliers had set foot on Umnak.

In August 1942, leadership of No. 111 was turned over to Squadron Leader Kenneth Boomer, an Ottawa native who had battled the Luftwaffe in the skies over Britain with two kills to his credit. In the meantime, the Americans had installed an air base on Adak Island. Situated near the centre of the Aleutian chain, it was 400 kilometres from Kiska and 640 kilometres from Attu. Japan had initially set her sights on Adak but opted against taking it due to the proximity of the Umnak airbase.

Boomer informed his men that a group of pilots from No. 111 would move out to Adak to participate in a direct combat mission against Japanese-held Kiska. Only one week after completion of the airstrip on Adak, five Canadian Kittyhawk fighters and an equal number of USAAF Aleutian Tigers (P-40 Warhawks) flew from Umnak to Adak to assume combat duties against Kiska.

On September 25, the first fighter-escorted bomber missions took place, with Major Jack Chennault leading the 343 Fighter Group of 12 Aleutian Tigers and four RCAF P-40s of the No. 111 under Squadron Leader Boomer. The fighters took off from Adak at 8:00 A.M. to make the treacherous 400-kilometre trip to Kiska. Overhead, the fighters rendezvoused with seven B-24 Liberators of the

36th Bombardment Squadron flying out of Cold Bay. Nearly two hours later, the Canadians regrouped east of Kiska.

The Liberators dropped their load of incendiaries and were followed by the fighters six minutes later. Owing to unusually clear weather, the Japanese spotted them with time to send up their two remaining "Rufes"—the float-fighter version of the deadly Zero. Pom-pom bursts of flak went up from Little Kiska, the small island sentinel in the harbour. At the Japanese seaplane base were some of the larger Japanese float planes—the big four-engine "Mavis" bombers, and "Pete" twin-wing reconnaissance planes. The fighters ripped through these as aircrews scrambled to get them airborne. Past the harbour, construction crews returning to work on a roughed-in airstrip dived for cover. Squadron Leader Boomer spotted a Rufe on the tail of an American Warhawk and laid into him with machine-gun fire. Boomer pulled back hard and, in his words, "climbed to a stall practically, pulled up right under him. I just poured it into him from underneath. He flamed up and went down." Jack Chennault brought the other Rufe corkscrewing down, trailing a plume of black smoke.

Both American and Canadian pilots who participated in the attack on Kiska were awarded the American Air Service Medal for their hazardous 800-kilometre, over-water flight. The RCAF pilots were Squadron Leader Ken Boomer, Pilot Officer H.O. Gooding and Flying Officers Robert Lynch and Jim Gohl—the latter an American who had joined to get his pilot training through the Commonwealth Air Training plan but stayed on in the RCAF. With his downing of the Rufe, Boomer earned the distinction of being the first Allied pilot to shoot down planes from both Germany and Japan.

The RCAF's No. 8 Bomber-Reconnaisance Squadron had extended its duties to Nome in July 1942, flying anti-submarine patrols over the Bering Sea as far as the Siberian coast. However, owing to the unlikelihood of submarine activity that far north and the lack of parts for the British-designed Bolingbroke, RCAF No. 14 Fighter Squadron out of Sea Island, Vancouver, was assigned to replace No. 8. The 15 Kittyhawks of No. 14 began the long trek north in February 1943. The squadron was grounded for four days at Port Hardy with some of the planes putting down at the remote Kwakwaka'wakw village of Alert Bay, which had a rough landing strip courtesy of the air force, and for nine days at Annette Island. Bypassing Yakutat because of fog, the squadron was forced to land at an emergency strip 130 kilometres away in Yakutaga. Four more days were lost ferrying fuel from Yakutat to Yakutaga, and bad weather continued to dog the flight from Anchorage to Cold Bay. No. 14 Squadron finally assembled at Umnak on March 18, a month after leaving Vancouver.

The Americans had roughed out an airstrip on Amchitka Island, only 110 kilometres east of Japanese-held Kiska. The two Canadian fighter squadrons rotated duties between providing anti-submarine coverage to Umnak and flying to the forward staging base at Adak and the combat front at

Crew members of RCAF No. 14 Fighter Squadron on Umnak Island. The pilots of 14 and 111 squadrons rotated between anti-submarine duty on Umnak and Kodiak and front-line combat at Amchitka Island. BERT MCCANN

Amchitka. Due to their short range, the P-40s were relegated strictly to missions against Kiska, only a short hop from Amchitka. The Kittyhawk wasn't fancy; in fact, veteran pilot Louis Cochand of St. Marguerite, Quebec, recalls that it was like flying a chunk of lead. Both American and Canadian models were configured to carry a 225-kilogram (500-pound) bomb strapped to the underbelly and were flown as dive-bombers. The modification brought its own unique problems, as Arthur Fanning, a Canadian P-40 pilot who flew combat over Kiska, recounts. Upon sighting the target, a P-40 pilot brought his plane into a steep bank at 4,000 metres; at 460 metres he reefed back on the elevator stick to release the bomb. The sudden release of the heavy payload while hauling back on the stick would send the plane hurtling skyward with enough G-force to render the pilot momentarily unconscious. Fanning explains, "You would come to, spinning wildly upward with no idea where you were before the plane was brought under control. That was the routine."

The P-40s concentrated on continually cratering the unfinished Japanese runway on Kiska, thereby denying the enemy the opportunity to station land-based fighters on the island. Other notable enemy targets were the anti-aircraft batteries, radar installations and the submarine and seaplane base. Even though the Japanese aircraft strength had been whittled down to nothing, they still threw up great amounts of flak at the marauding planes. However, the horrendous Aleutian weather caused greater concern than the flak as pilots were unsure if they could find the Amchitka runway in the fog after returning from Kiska.

At its peak, the RCAF provided one-fifth of all combined air forces in Alaska, and 11 RCAF pilots of No. 14 and No. 111 squadrons received the American Air Medal. Both squadrons returned to Canada in September 1943 and went on to distinguish themselves in the skies over Europe. No. 111 was redesignated No. 440 Squadron (Typhoons) and No. 14 became No. 442 Squadron (Spitfires).

9

The Battle of the Komandorski Islands

BY EARLY 1943, THE COLD northern islands of volcanic rock that many in Japan's military had previously thought to be useless were now crucial to Japan's survival. The Aleutians were all that stood in the way of an all-out Allied assault on the home islands from the north. While the Aleutians served as potential stepping stones to North America, their strategic location also worked against Japan. A loss of Japan's holdings in the Aleutians would allow the Allies to establish bases close enough for an air attack on Paramushiro, a navy base in northern Japan, and possibly allow them to push farther south to Japan's major industrial cities. A large naval force could then follow the bombers from the Aleutians.

Although possession of the Aleutians could give either side an advantage, both had given them low priority. The war in Alaska had become a costly diversion as both Japan and the United States saw the deployment of aircraft, munitions and troops to the Aleutians as secondary to maintaining a tentative hold on territory in the South Pacific and other fronts. For the Allies, at least, supply lines were improved by the completion of the Alaska Highway and the lack of an effective Japanese submarine offensive against West Coast shipping.

In January 1943, the Americans set up a blockade of the western Aleutians under the command of Rear Admiral Charles H. McMorris. He had come to Attu Island's Holtz Bay when an American submarine had reported several enemy ships anchored there. McMorris steamed off in his flagship, the cruiser *Richmond*, along with *Indianapolis* and four destroyers. A rare break in the weather allowed McMorris to reach Attu hours ahead of the estimated time, only to find that either the submarine reports were wrong or the enemy had given them the slip. McMorris decided that even if the enemy had no ships in the area, he could rattle the Japanese encamped on Attu. From eight kilometres offshore, the big guns of *Indianapolis* and *Richmond* pounded Chichagof Village on Holtz Bay. The shelling killed 23 soldiers and shattered some of the Aleut wooden buildings being used by the Japanese. After a two-hour barrage, McMorris withdrew his ships to the waters between

Japan's northern Kurile Islands and the western Aleutians. It was time to turn up the heat on the enemy.

With such a small contingent of warships, it was reasoned that the only effective use of force would be a naval blockade of the islands. The strategy was to intercept enemy vessels attempting to resupply the Aleutian bases and thereby starve the Japanese out of Alaska.

Loaded with supplies and fresh troops, the transport ship *Akagane Maru* was the first to run afoul of the blockade when the *Indianapolis* easily sank it as it headed to Attu. In the following days, the American fleet forced more than a dozen other supply ships to return to Japan. By March 1943, the Japanese had lost or suffered damage to more than 40 ships supporting the Alaskan garrisons. When a transport went down, small gifts and personal letters from loved ones back home were lost along with the supplies of food, spare parts and equipment.

Lieutenant General Kiichiro Higuchi, commander of all Japanese land forces of the empire's northern possessions, could see that McMorris's blockade was strangling his vital supply line to the Aleutians. Seeing the navy as the only hope for his beleaguered Alaskan garrisons, he prevailed on them to deal directly with the blockade. On March 22, Admiral Hosogaya responded by ordering the heavy cruisers *Maya* and *Nachi*; light cruisers *Akubunka* and *Tama*; destroyers *Wakab*, *Hatsushimo*, *Ikazuchi*, *Usagumo* and *Inazuma*; and transports *Maru Sanko*, *Maru Sakito* and

Maru Asaka from Paramushiro. It was time to smash through the American fleet.

On the morning of March 26, Admiral McMorris's blockade of ships—his own ship, *Richmond*, heavy cruiser *Salt Lake City*, which had just replaced *Indianapolis*, and destroyers *Monaghan*, *Dale*, *Bailey* and *Coghlan*—were 160 kilometres south of Russia's Komandorski Islands, a 600-kilometre extension of the Aleutian Island chain on the Bering Sea.

From high up in the *Richmond*'s crow's nest, the lookout reported five vessels—mere specks on the horizon topped by columns of smoke. As the alarm bell brought the ships about face to confront the enemy, McMorris believed he would only be engaging an enemy supply convoy. Alerted by his bridge officers to approaching ships on the southern horizon, Admiral Hosogaya ordered the launch of Pete aircraft to verify the ships' origin. Receiving confirmation that they were indeed the American blockade ships positioning for battle, Hosogaya changed course to broadside the enemy fleet. His ships outweighed and outgunned the American boats by a ratio of two to one, and from a point 11 kilometres off they opened fire with 250-millimetre (10-inch) guns and bracketed the cruiser *Richmond* with towering water geysers.

Salt Lake City replied with its forward gun turret, landing shells just below *Nachi*'s bridge and knocking out power to the forward turret. *Nachi*'s electricians soon had the turret back in action, but almost as quickly, *Salt Lake City* scored three more hits on *Nachi* in the same vicinity. This time, power to the main guns as well as the bridge was cut, the main mast was wrenched askew and three officers on the bridge were killed, with Hosogaya himself narrowly escaping death. Return fire from the Japanese cruisers landed shells squarely on *Salt Lake City*'s main deck, crashing below into the engine room and buckling a watertight bulkhead. A defect within the cruiser's steam-powered steering system, resulting from firing the ship's big guns, had already reduced the *Salt Lake City*'s manoeuvrability, and now sea water seeped in through the damaged hull plating and threatened to short out the main generators. Noting the cruiser's speed had dropped to a few knots, the Japanese force formed an ever-tightening arc with their guns fixed on their quarry.

Salt Lake City took a heavy shot below the waterline, and the icy North Pacific began welling up and shorting out fuses in the port side engine room and adjoining compartments. The switchboard room, aft steering room, aft ammunition compartment and shaft alleys three and four were flooded. Fuel oil, hydraulic fluid and oil from a ruptured lubricating-oil tank swirled around ladders and fittings. Soon its engines stopped.

Other ships of the Alaskan fleet pulled in closer to put up a defensive smoke screen around *Salt Lake City* to obscure its position. It had run up three signal flags indicating "MY SPEED ZERO" after salt water in its fuel valves choked off the propulsion machinery and quenched the steam boilers. In the engine room, engineers and oilers worked to purge the contaminated fuel from the supply lines and switch over to the starboard fuel tanks, which were still not breached. The cruiser was also listing five degrees to port, and the gun crews had expended all of the large-bore ammunition. Two men were dead and several wounded. McMorris considered ordering the *Salt Lake City*'s crew to abandon ship, but that would leave *Richmond* open to the four Japanese cruisers.

The battle raged for nearly four hours, and the Japanese also made direct hits on *Bailey* with their 200-millimetre (8-inch) guns as the American destroyer attempted to divert action from the stricken *Salt Lake City*. It was now only a matter of delivering the coup de grâce to the damaged cruiser, but the Japanese, believing American bombers from Adak were surely on their way and having no air cover of their own, broke off the attack and retreated west. It was a lost opportunity for Hosogaya. Despite the American navy's request for air support, the army bombers remained idle on the airfield at Adak, their bombs frozen to the ground.

Upon returning to Japan, Admiral Hosogaya was relieved of command for his poor assessment of the naval engagement and subsequent withdrawal from battle. For the remainder of his career, he was relegated to the naval reserve. Admiral McMorris claimed a victory, and the Battle of the Komandorski Islands went down in history as the longest naval artillery duel in modern naval warfare and the last "big ship" duel of the Second World War.

10

Attu: 19 Days of Hell

ON JUNE 7, 1942, FOLLOWING THE two attacks on Dutch Harbor, Japanese troops had occupied Kiska and Attu, the westernmost islands of Alaska's remote and barren Aleutian chain. This became the only piece of North America occupied by an enemy force during the Second World War.

On Attu, the village of 43 Aleut Natives and two white residents was surrounded by 1,200 Japanese soldiers. Etta Jones was the village schoolteacher, and her husband Foster maintained a weather-monitoring station. Foster Jones was executed by Japanese army troops, while Etta and the Aleut were sent to internment camps in Japan.

Ten men at the US Navy weather station were the only inhabitants of Kiska when 500 Japanese Navy Landing

Force troops came ashore in the early hours and wracked the weather station with machine-gun fire. The Americans all scattered but were soon caught except for one man. William Charles House managed to elude the Japanese by hiding out in the caves of Kiska eating grass and worms. After 51 days, the cold and emaciated House surrendered.

Kiska became the bastion of the Japanese possessions in Alaska with 7,200 Imperial Navy troops and 1,800 soldiers of the Imperial Army. Attu had a garrison of 2,800 Imperial soldiers. Life in the Aleutians was hard for the Japanese troops as they endured cold weather, constant fog and relentless winds that blew over 100 kilometres per hour.

To counter the Japanese advance in the Aleutians, the Americans installed USAAF and US Navy bases down the Aleutian chain as far west as Amchitka Island, located only 105 kilometres east of Japanese-held Kiska. This allowed the USAAF and US Navy to subject Kiska and Attu to terrific bombing campaigns. In March 1943, the American navy blockaded the Japanese-held islands, culminating in the Battle of the Komadorski Islands.

At the Casablanca Conference in January 1943, British prime minister Winston Churchill and American president Franklin Roosevelt approved plans to recapture the occupied Alaskan islands. As the main enemy base in the Aleutians, Kiska was originally the first target; however, the Allies ultimately favoured retaking the smaller island of Attu first, since this would leave Kiska in the centre of a pincer movement and vulnerable to a greater concentration of forces.

For the assault, General John DeWitt requested the 32nd Infantry Division under Major General Charles H. Corlett and General Eugene Landrum, both of whom already had experience in the Aleutians. DeWitt instead received the 7th Infantry Motorized Division, which had just completed desert-warfare training in California and was destined for the war in North Africa. The unit was commanded by Major General Albert E. Brown, a career soldier who had gained combat experience in the trenches of France in the First World War. DeWitt protested that a mechanized unit would prove useless in the Aleutians, where muskeg and hilly terrain would cause wheeled and tracked vehicles to bog down. Every piece of equipment and all supplies moving to the front line would have to be packed in on the backs of men, he argued, and an infantry unit was the only viable option. He was overruled but found support from Admiral Kinkaid, who held that if a desert unit was to be used, it should at least be commanded by someone with knowledge of the Aleutians. DeWitt and Kinkaid's protests again came to nothing, and General Brown's command was affirmed.

To safeguard the secrecy of the upcoming invasion, the soldiers of the 7th Division were led to believe they were headed for a battlefield in the tropics. After training in amphibious landings on the beaches of California, in conditions completely opposite to those of the Aleutians, they shipped out 10,000 strong from San Diego, thinking that they were bound for the Solomon Islands in the South Pacific. Loaded aboard were crates of gear marked "Australia." After a two-week cramped trip in five transports up the stormy coast of the Pacific Northwest, they arrived in Cold Bay, Alaska.

On April 18, Japan suffered another in a succession of devastating losses. Admiral Isoroku Yamamoto, the great naval strategist who planned Pearl Harbor and almost solely directed the Japanese destiny in the Pacific, was assassinated while touring his South Pacific bases on a morale-building exercise. After American code breakers determined his itinerary, P-38s ambushed his plane and sent it down in flames into the jungle of Rabul.

News of the admiral's death was a particularly serious blow to the morale of Japanese troops on Attu. All contact with the homeland, apart from radio, was gone, and food, medical goods and even such basics as kindling were in very short supply. The Americans stepped up their harassment of the island as the day of invasion approached. In one week alone, 90,000 kilograms (198,400 pounds) of bombs fell on the tiny outpost, although most failed to do any damage other than unnerve the Japanese, and the weather often forced the planes to dump their load onto the now secondary target of Kiska. This increased activity helped confirm the Japanese belief that Kiska was the primary

Allied objective, as by now they were well aware that the US was building up resources for an assault.

Attu, the focus of all this frenzied activity, was little more than a barren heap of moss-covered rock, standing alone at the western extremity of Alaska's Aleutian chain. Only 30 kilometres at its widest point and 64 kilometres long, it reaches 914 metres above sea level at its highest peaks. Colonel Yasuyo Yamasaki, who had arrived on Attu in April by float plane, faced the impossible task of holding this lonely outpost at all costs with fewer than 2,000 troops left of his 303rd Independent Infantry Battalion and no hope of reinforcements until late May. His best defence lay in commanding the steep ridges above Holtz and Massacre Valleys, 3,000 metres inland at the head of the bays. By moving his men, mobile guns, mortars and machine guns to the high ground from the two main defence sectors at Holtz Bay and Chichagof, he planned to force the invaders to make their way up the valleys to reach the Japanese encampments.

While Japanese troops in the jungles of Asia and the South Pacific could use the dense tropical foliage as camouflage, the Alaskan tundra afforded no such protection. Instead, Yamasaki's men dotted the terrain with foxholes and dug two-man mortar and machine-gun posts into the muskeg, from which the Japanese weapons, although not highly accurate, would give off no flash to betray their position. A few well-hidden men in posts positioned throughout the terrain could pin down superior numbers of men. Yamasaki may have hoped his soldiers could fight a delaying action long enough for promised reinforcements to arrive from Japan or Kiska.

At Cold Bay, the men of the 7th Division were sequestered in the convoy ships that had brought them to Alaska since there was no room to house them on land. The desert army was given no opportunity to train on Aleutian beaches for amphibious landings, and all available cold-weather gear had been consigned to Europe, leaving them without suitable clothing. Many of the men were from America's Southwest and had not even seen snow before. Now, with neither proper training nor equipment, they were to go into battle against a Japanese army well accustomed to the deprivations of the Aleutians.

By late April 1943, the American invasion force had moved west into the islands and dispersed at bases along the Aleutian chain, spread out over hundreds of kilometres as no one place was large enough to accommodate the influx of troops. The force comprised members of the Alaska Scouts, the 7th, 17th and 32nd infantry divisions (with the 4th Infantry Regiment held in reserve), four artillery battalions, an engineering battalion and supporting units of medical and service personnel. The American ground troops totalled almost 20,000 men—surely adequate to dislodge 1,600 starving Japanese soldiers.

Naval support consisted of the battleships *Nevada* and

Pennsylvania, salvaged from the carnage of Pearl Harbor, the battleship *Idaho* and an escort force of six cruisers, nineteen destroyers and an aircraft carrier. Together with McMorris's blockade fleet of three cruisers and six destroyers, as well as a phalanx of army and navy aircraft, they steamed west to Attu on May 4.

At 1:00 A.M. on May 11, in heavy fog and with the temperature standing at -12°C, 244 scouts from two combat units disembarked from the submarines *Narwhal* and *Nautilus* and paddled for Austin Cove on Attu's northeast shore. There, the two units split into two platoons each and filed out toward the mountains that separated them from Holtz and Massacre Bays, where the main assault forces would land. In their packs were only enough rations for 36 hours.

For the rest of the day, the scouts followed a creek up the steep slope of the first range that peaked over Holtz Valley. By nightfall, two groups had made it to the mountaintop, where they bivouacked in the fog. Subzero temperatures and a heavy covering of snow made for a shivering, sleepless night. At dawn, the two groups began their descent into the valley, out of sight of each other and communicating using runners in order to avoid alerting the enemy to their presence. As they slid down the snow-covered slopes, laughing at the absurdity of it all like schoolboys given a snow day, Japanese snipers opened with sporadic machine-gun and artillery fire. Shooting back as they went, the four platoons continued their advance into the canyon but were solidly

US Army troops landed on Attu on May 10, 1943. Some 549 Americans were killed in the 19-day battle against desperate Japanese soldiers. BRENDAN COYLE COLLECTION

pinned down by late afternoon. Any scout who showed his head drew a burst of machine-gun fire, while the Japanese moved freely about.

By afternoon on May 12, the scouts of the 7th brought up their 81-millimetre (3-inch) mortar and sent the advancing Japanese pulling back into the protective wall of the valley. From positions on the hill, however, Japanese gunners kept the scouts hunkered down throughout the night and into the next day. A supply plane droned overhead in the fog, then turned away, unable to spot the scout groups, which by now had nearly depleted their rations. In the late afternoon, scouts of the 7th Cavalry Reconnaissance made their way into the canyon to join the advance party, and by nightfall, using their combined strength, they managed to drive the enemy back temporarily. The Japanese quickly regrouped and again tied down the Americans by machine-gun fire.

The scouts burrowed into the snow to shelter their wounded and made tiny fires of ration wrappers in an attempt to keep warm. Through the darkness, through bursts of machine-gun fire that bounced off the canyon walls above, they could hear insults hurled in broken English: "Damn American dogs, we kill you . . . we massacre you."

Well into the afternoon of May 12, the main Attu invasion force still bobbed around the island's east shore. They had had trouble finding the shore because of the dense fog, but finally a radar-equipped craft announced the beach was ahead. A second boat followed to undertake the American's army's first-ever amphibious invasion. With one assault force landing at Red Beach, just north of Holtz Bay, and another at Massacre Bay, 13 kilometres south, separated by mountainous terrain, the plan was to trap the main Japanese force in a pincer movement on the peninsula at Chichagof. In a tactic typical of the Japanese, the landings were unopposed in order to draw the invaders inland, where they would face a well-entrenched Japanese force.

Company F landed on the beach at Massacre Bay and headed north into the mountains. Between the rocky shore and the incline of the mountains lay a few thousand metres of spongy tundra covered in deep snow. The men sank to their hips with their first steps. The volcanic slopes rising from Massacre Bay's shores were so steep in places that the invaders had to use ropes to haul up their weapons. They spent the evening and night working their way into the valley heading toward Clevesy Pass. By daybreak, the Japanese had formed a horseshoe in front of the Americans, closing off their entrance route. The men of Company F had not slept since their landing at Massacre Bay two days before and were sick from hunger and exhaustion. Through sheer determination, the squads made it up the north slope of the valley and regrouped.

Meanwhile, the forces attempting to land to the north at Red Beach were harassed by Japanese artillery until army bombers roared in and saturated the enemy with 45-kilogram (100-pound) bombs, allowing 4,000 troops to land. Once ashore they encountered problems with terrain, as their 105-millimetre (4-inch) howitzers became bogged down less than 100 metres from shore.

Days after landing on Attu, following strafing by wildcat fighter planes and on-the-ground combat, the Americans still had not made a dent in the enemy's defences. In addition, the northern (Holtz Bay) and southern (Massacre Bay) American forces had not linked up as planned. The strategy had called for Attu to be taken in three days, but even after five days of fighting the Japanese had not given up an inch of ground.

In an attempt to dislodge the enemy, the battleships *Pennsylvania* and *Nevada* pounded the Japanese on the hills for two and a half hours, but to no avail. A break in the impasse finally occurred when an observer crept unseen to within sight of the Japanese camp and directed the 350-millimetre (14-inch) guns from the battleship *Idaho*, which tore the encampment apart. The Americans in the north were now able to advance into the valley for the first time since the landing; however, the Japanese fell back toward Chichagof to take up positions on each succeeding ridge and begin the standoff all over again.

Private William Jones, made squadron leader because his senior NCOs had all been killed, gave his first order, directing a soldier to advance while other soldiers covered him. The man took a bullet and later died in Jones's arms. That same day, Jones received news that the dead soldier was a 38-year-old father of seven who had been mistakenly sent to the front. He was to have been immediately sent home due to his age and family status.

All supplies to the front lines on Attu had to be packed in, sourdough style, on the backs of men, 25 kilograms at a time. Eventually road-building equipment was brought in to plough up a creek, which relieved the large number of men serving as pack animals. The transfer of men and equipment to and from the transport ships slowed to a trickle, however, as only three of the 93 original landing craft were still in operation. Most had come to grief on Attu's treacherous approaches. Some became swamped and went straight to the bottom, drowning their load of troops or wounded.

As the Japanese withdrew from the north of the island, Company B of the 17th Infantry followed them across Holtz Valley. In gritty hand-to-hand fighting, the company took many casualties before driving the Japanese off the ridge. As the drifting fog cleared, the navy fighters from *Nassau* flew over; unaware the hill had just changed hands, they strafed their own men.

The northern force continued its push on the Japanese. By now, more than 12,500 American troops were on the island, while the Japanese now numbered fewer than 1,000 capable soldiers. On May 18, patrols from the northern and southern forces finally linked up, closing the arc, and turned eastward to push the Japanese onto the Chichagof Peninsula with their backs against the sea.

The Americans launched a coordinated assault on both flanks of the pass in the morning of May 19. Three patrols of Americans fought the terrain and elements as well as the Japanese. One patrol clawed up Cold Mountain, where the barren slopes offered little cover to conceal the advancing troops. They opened the attack by lobbing grenades into the enemy camp, but the grenades rolled harmlessly down the steep slope and only served to alert the enemy. Fog rolled in and obscured the enemy position, and when it lifted the Americans found themselves almost face to face with the Japanese soldiers. Point Able finally fell to the Americans on May 20. Typical of the Japanese fighting spirit, every Imperial soldier died defending it.

By May 23, thousands more American soldiers had poured into Attu, while Yamasaki was down to 800 able bodies and 600 wounded, his back to the sea and facing the enemy on three sides. His men had totally depleted their food and ammunition supplies, and he had received word from home that there would be no relief until perhaps early July. Leaflets dropped by American bombers called for surrender, but this was out of the question for Yamasaki. He would fight to the death, if necessary, as he had one last plan. He would mount frontal banzai attacks to capture weapons and supplies, buying time until reinforcements arrived, and hope the Americans would eventually withdraw.

All the Japanese wounded who were too incapacitated to walk or fight were gathered into bomb craters. There, they were given a dose of morphine and a blessing before hand grenades were tossed among them to spare them the disgrace of capture. Yamasaki's battered army then moved off in the early morning of May 28 to stealthily attack Company B of the 32nd Infantry, catching the Americans off guard. The Japanese fought frantically, shooting and thrusting bayonets. The Americans scattered and withdrew to the command post of the 2nd Battalion 17th Infantry. The news of a Japanese counterattack was hard to believe, but almost immediately the command post was also swarmed by the Japanese.

At a medical evacuation station across from Engineer

Hill, an American stronghold, men were awakened by the sound of gunshots. Grenades exploded outside their tents as a screaming mob of Japanese soldiers ripped through the tents, demanding grenades and cigarettes with their few words of English. A force of American soldiers arrived in pursuit, and the Japanese retreated in a hail of bullets.

A medical clearing station had been set up at the base of Engineer Hill. Shortly after 4:00 A.M., the calm of the tent was broken when the company quartermaster burst inside yelling, "The Japs are coming!" Outside the tent, the Japanese descended upon the stacks of rifles belonging to the wounded, and their excited chatter filtered inside.

The wounded Americans in the tent held their breath, waiting for the Japanese to come through the flaps. One Japanese soldier pulled back the canvas door but withdrew in disgust at the sight of a dead patient's shattered head. Then another came looking for food. The Americans played dead and were relieved when he was called back outside. The men trapped inside remained still throughout the whole day and into the next morning, their fate resting on the few steps it would take for the Japanese to venture inside for a serious look.

The following morning, the American soldiers on the hill who had been scattered by the Japanese regrouped to form a defensive line against the enemy and began fighting fiercely to force them back. But the Japanese continued to mount attacks throughout the day, albeit in ever-dwindling numbers. Finally, the tattered remnants of the Japanese force realized they were facing certain defeat with no hope of rescue. Most committed suicide by putting grenades to their temples; Yamasaki had died earlier, sword in hand. By the time the Japanese abandoned the camp, the Americans trapped inside the medical tent had lain motionless for the better part of a day. The surviving Americans burst into a chorus of yelling as soldiers from their own side approached, preparing to lob grenades into the tent.

The battle for Attu officially ended after 19 days of brutal fighting when the Americans moved into Chichagof on May 30, although small pockets of Japanese resistance had to be mopped up well into June. Many of the remaining Japanese soldiers took their own lives. Of the original 2,800 Japanese on Attu, only 26 were taken prisoner. The Americans lost 549 servicemen in the battle. They are interred at Fort Richardson Cemetery near Anchorage.

While the defeat at Attu ended Japanese hopes of invading Alaska through the Aleutians, it did not mean the end of attacks on the US homeland. A Japanese invasion of a very different sort would soon have tragic consequences in an American state far to the south.

11

Balloons of War

ON SUNDAY, MAY 5, 1945, in Bly, Oregon, Pastor Archie Mitchell drove with his wife Elsye, who was five months pregnant, and five children from his congregation to Gearhart Mountain in the Fremont National Forest for a day of picnicking and hiking. Upon arrival, Mitchell let his wife and the children out while he parked the car. Shortly after, Mrs. Mitchell called to her husband from about 95 metres away, saying that they had found something. Suddenly, a terrific explosion engulfed the group, killing Elyse and all the children. Their tragic discovery had been a *fugo*, or *fusen bakudan*, a Japanese army balloon bomb. Sadly, both the Canadian and American governments knew that the balloon bombs had reached their shores, but had kept quiet about them so that Japanese intelligence would not know of their effectiveness. The six deaths in Oregon finally prompted those same governments to issue public warnings about the devices.

In November 1944, the Imperial Army and Navy had conducted a series of tests that sent balloons carrying recording and transmitting instruments to North America. Aware of a constant jet stream high in the stratosphere that moved from west to east, the Japanese embarked on a program to send armed balloons as unguided missiles against North America. Japanese scientists determined that with a moderate payload of less than 170 kilograms, a balloon could ride eight kilometres above the ocean's surface, which put it beyond the reach of radar and most aircraft patrols. Travelling at speeds of up to 480 kilometres per hour, it could cross the Pacific from Japan to North America in about three days.

The balloons were made of laminated paper panels shellacked together by schoolgirls with a type of potato paste. Food was now so scarce in Japan that supervisors at the balloon factory had to be on guard for workers who would steal the paste to eat. Initial production of the balloons took place in scattered small-scale locations, such as school halls, judo dojos and auditoriums, before more permanent quarters were established at the Kokura Arsenal on Kyushu.

Measuring 10 metres in diameter and 21.3 metres from

top to bottom, the fully inflated balloons held 6,100 cubic metres of explosive hydrogen gas for lifting. They were equipped with a pressure-relief valve that released air as the balloon drifted between higher and lower pressures at different altitudes, and they could reach a height of 10,000 metres. Sixteen-metre lines suspended the weapon, which consisted of two aluminum rings with a series of 75 blow plugs. Batteries, barometers and altimeters controlled gunpowder charges that intermittently released 16 pairs of sandbags being used as ballast. By the time the balloons were over North America, ideally they would have released all of their sandbags. The devices were armed with four 5-kilogram (11-pound) magnesium incendiaries for starting random fires in forests. They were also equipped with a 15-kilogram (33-pound) anti-personnel bomb designed to kill civilians should it land in an urban area. A one-kilogram (2.2-pound) picric-acid block would destroy the remains of the device and evidence of its country of origin, as it burned very hot and was a suitable fire starter. The magnesium flash powder would then ignite the remaining hydrogen in the balloon.

Picric acid is a highly explosive compound with properties similar to TNT. It had been used in the First World War but fell out of favour due to its instability. This instability was proven when a ship carrying 2,300 tons of picric acid, as well as TNT, blew up in Halifax in 1917, killing 1,900 in the largest man-made explosion up to that date. The Halifax

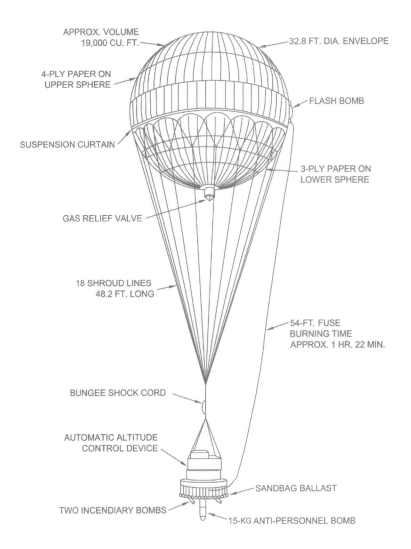

APPROX. VOLUME
19,000 CU. FT.

32.8 FT. DIA. ENVELOPE

4-PLY PAPER ON
UPPER SPHERE

FLASH BOMB

SUSPENSION CURTAIN

3-PLY PAPER ON
LOWER SPHERE

GAS RELIEF VALVE

18 SHROUD LINES
48.2 FT. LONG

54-FT. FUSE
BURNING TIME
APPROX. 1 HR. 22 MIN.

BUNGEE SHOCK CORD

AUTOMATIC ALTITUDE
CONTROL DEVICE

SANDBAG BALLAST

TWO INCENDIARY BOMBS

15-KG ANTI-PERSONNEL BOMB

The *fusen bakudan*, Japanese balloon bombs, were launched to spread terror on the west coast of North America. The above diagram shows the construction and features of a balloon bomb.

TOBY FRANKLEN

explosion was studied by nuclear scientist Robert Oppenheimer to estimate the power of the atomic bombs being developed for use against Japan. As well as for its explosive ability, picric acid was also used in the early 20th century as an antiseptic and to treat burns. It had been used to treat the victims of the Hindenburg disaster in 1937, only a few years earlier. Picric acid is still used in fireworks today, as it emits a high pitched whine during combustion in air.

The Allies, who at the time were unaware of the existence of the jet stream, initially had no idea where the strange devices originated. It was unthinkable that they could come from Japan, more than 8,000 kilometres away. Many theories were put forward, among them the thought that they had been delivered by enemy submarines off the West Coast or even by landing parties on the very beaches of North America. Some suggested that the balloon bombs were secretly deployed from camps in which Nikkei, or second-generation Japanese, had been interned, while others more accurately thought that they came from South Pacific atolls.

From the markings on the metal components and paper balloon fragments, it was already known that the weapons were Japanese. Gradually, the military also realized that the weapons were indeed launched from Japan. Samples of the balloon's ballast sand were sent to Ottawa. A.E. Porsild, a government botanist, extracted pine needles, sedge seeds and a few rice grains from the sand. None of the plant samples were native to North America, but they did grow in

Japan. A Canadian geologist with the Department of Mines and Resources also dissected the sand and found minute traces of metal slag, the residue from a very particular type of blast furnace. Tiny globules of melted steel clinging to the slag confirmed it was from a steel mill, and records showed that the Japanese had operated two steel mills that used this type of process furnace.

The Military Geology Unit of the United States Geological Survey also worked on finding the source of the weapons and pinpointing exactly where in Japan the balloons originated. They began a forensic examination worthy of the best criminologists. With the assistance of geologists, paleontologists, micropaleontologists, mineralogists and petrologists, the survey team painstakingly analyzed the sand in the recovered ballast bags. They narrowed the search to beaches with rivers flowing from sources having the same ratios of mineral concentration as the sand. The team also discovered the sand to have no coral, indicating that the river source was in cold waters above the 35th parallel—roughly the same latitude as San Francisco. Signs of granite further narrowed the water to inland streams that meandered through bedrock, while grains of quartz, augite and glass were evidence of a volcanic region. Minute crustaceans and fossils native to a very confined area of Japan's east coast were also pulled from the sand samples. Slowly and steadily, scientific deductions narrowed the whereabouts of the balloon-bomb factory to three sites on the east coast of Honshu, northeast of Tokyo. Each had rail lines and an arsenal for storage of the weapons, as well as hydrogen generators and storage tanks for the hydrogen.

About 9,300 *fusen bakudan* were launched against North America, landing as far north as the Yukon Territory, as far east as Michigan and south into Mexico. British Columbia recorded 57 balloon bombs shot down or recovered, the most of any province or state. Two were sighted over Port Hardy, one of which was brought down by gunfire while the other escaped. Two intact five-kilogram (11-pound) bombs were recovered with their ballast gear on Denman Island, near Courtenay, and in 1978, loggers found the remains of another exploded balloon bomb in the coastal forest near Agness, Oregon. Bombs also landed in Williams Lake, Boundary Bay, the Gulf Islands, the Strait of Georgia, the Queen Charlotte Islands and Prince Rupert. Cowboys reported one in the Thompson River valley near Ashcroft, and another crashed into Vancouver's Coal Harbour near the entrance to Stanley Park. The last balloon bomb was shot down on April 20, 1945, near the Huntingdon–Sumas border crossing, after two children spotted it through a break in the clouds. A P-40 Kittyhawk piloted by P.V. Brodeur scrambled out of the RCAF base at Abbotsford and brought it down for a joint Canadian–American investigating team to recover intact.

Almost 50 more balloons or their remains were found in Alberta, Saskatchewan, Manitoba, Yukon and the

Northwest Territories, while the coastal states of California, Oregon, Washington and Alaska recorded a total of 135 incidents. On March 10, 1945, a balloon bomb caused a power outage for three days at the Hanford Engineer Works, the nuclear production facility that produced the plutonium used in the atomic bomb dropped on Nagasaki. The three-day power outage caused by the balloon bomb did little to slow down production.

In May 1945, American B29 Superfortress bombers took out two of the three balloon-bomb production facilities at Ichinomiya, Nakoso and Otsu. Between the bombing and the lack of feedback from the American media as to the effectiveness of the balloon bombs, the Japanese decision makers cancelled the program, unaware that more than 300 balloon bombs or parts had been reported or recovered in Canada and the United States. Thousands more likely crashed into remote forests, and their remains have been discovered as recently as 1992. While the Allies speculated that the Japanese would eventually use the balloon bombs to transport chemical or biological weapons, no enemy data uncovered after the war supports that theory.

Epilogue

FOLLOWING THE JAPANESE LOSS ON Attu, a joint American–Canadian assault force of 35,000 troops landed on Kiska on August 15, 1943. It had been estimated that 8,500 starving Japanese were holed up in the bleak hills of Kiska, but when the Allied force landed, the enemy was nowhere to be found. On July 28, undetected under cover of fog, a large Japanese evacuation force had removed the entire 5,500-man Kiska garrison in one of the most successful rescue missions of the whole war. Twenty-five Americans and four Canadians were killed by friendly fire or by enemy booby traps planted by the retreating Japanese.

After Japan's retreat, the RCAF squadrons posted to Alaska and northern BC were redeployed overseas, where they distinguished themselves in the skies over Europe. While Japan's withdrawal had diminished the threat to the coast, sporadic enemy incursions still occurred. Submarine I-180 sank the freighter *John Straub* off Unimak Island in April 1944. One week later, I-180 itself was sunk south of Kodiak Island. Japanese sub I-12 was badly damaged 160 kilometres west-southwest of Los Angeles in November 1944 while shadowing a six-ship convoy. It was sunk two months later in the same area where *Cynthia Olson* met her end three years earlier.

The war had devastating and lasting effects on some West Coast residents. For reasons of security, thousands of Nikkei, second-generation North American Japanese, had their properties expropriated and were sent to holding camps in the interior. Just what level of threat was posed by these citizens is still hotly debated. Over 40 years later, both Canada and the United States offered an official apology and compensation for their governments' wartime actions.

The Hanford Nuclear Plant that produced plutonium for the war has left a toxic environmental impact. It has been declared the most contaminated site in the western hemisphere. A massive multi-billion dollar and multi-faceted long-term cleanup has begun; however, this legacy of war will endure for many more decades.

Fortunately, other legacies of the war on the West Coast have been beneficial. Today, thousands of people travel the Alaska Highway without giving any thought to the dramatic events that served as the impetus for its construction and the political machinations it took for the massive project to come to fruition. The highway is merely a means of travel from British Columbia to the wilds of the North; the "Highway to Tokyo" moniker is forgotten, and the men who toiled to build it in freezing temperatures and harsh conditions have faded into memory.

Since the end of the Second World War, the Pacific Coast Militia Rangers, re-formed as the Canadian Rangers, have remained vigilant. In 2003, Canada Post issued a 48-cent domestic-rate stamp to honour the Rangers. The stamp is a tribute to their motto of "Vigilans" or "the watchers" and features a close-up of a red-capped Ranger looking through binoculars with snowy mountains reflected in the lenses.

* * *

In Oregon, on Delaura Beach Lane, near Fort Stevens, a monument stands testament to Meiji Tagami's daring raid on the fort. It is situated at one of the craters from his bombs and reads:

> On June 21, 1942 a 5.5" shell exploded here, one of 17 fired at Columbia River harbor defense installations by the Japanese submarine I-25, the only hostile shelling of a military base on the U.S. mainland during World War II and the first since the War of 1812.

Epilogue

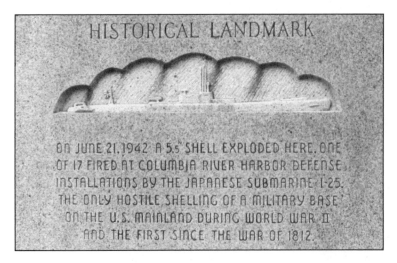

HISTORICAL LANDMARK

ON JUNE 21, 1942 A 5.5" SHELL EXPLODED HERE. ONE OF 17 FIRED AT COLUMBIA RIVER HARBOR DEFENSE INSTALLATIONS BY THE JAPANESE SUBMARINE I-25. THE ONLY HOSTILE SHELLING OF A MILITARY BASE ON THE U.S. MAINLAND DURING WORLD WAR II AND THE FIRST SINCE THE WAR OF 1812.

This monument marks the site where one of 17 shells fired by Japanese submarine I-25 landed only metres short of the Hitchmen family home near Fort Stevens, Oregon, on June 21, 1942.

BRENDAN COYLE

Warrant Officer Fujita never did burn down an American forest with his incendiary bombs; however he took pride in the fact that he had struck directly at the enemy's homeland. Fifty years later, on September 9, 1992, Nobuo Fujita returned to Oregon at the age of 80 to plant a tree at the site of his first bombing, now within Siskiyou National Forest, and presented his family's 400-year-old samurai sword to the City of Brookings. Fujita was made an honorary citizen of Brookings several days before his death in Japan on September 30, 1997, at the age of 85 and his daughter, Yoriko Asakura, buried some of Fujita's ashes at the bomb site.

Bibliography

Brown, G.I. *The Big Bang: A History of Explosives*. London: Sutton Publishing, 1998.

Canada. Department of National Defence. "*Canadian Rangers*." www.army.forces.gc.ca/land-terre/cr-rc/index-eng.asp.

Canada Post. "Canadian Rangers." *Canada's Stamp Details XII, no. 1 (January–March 2003)*, www.canadapost.ca/cpo/mc/personal/ collecting/stamps/archives/2003/2003_feb_rangers.jsf.

CFB Esquimalt Naval & Military Museum. "Pacific Coast Militia Rangers." www.navalandmilitarymuseum.org/resource_pages/ coastal_defence/pcmr.html.

Chandonnet, Fern. *Alaska at War 1941–1945: The Forgotten War Remembered*. Fairbanks: University of Alaska Press, 2008.

Coyle, Brendan. *War on our Doorstep: The Unknown Campaign on North America's West Coast*. Surrey, BC: Heritage House, 2002.

"Special Forces." canadiansoldiers.com. www.canadiansoldiers.com/ organization/specialforces/specialforces.htm.

Tourism Dawson Creek. "Alaska Highway." www.tourismdawsoncreek. com/index.php/alaskahighway.php.

Tucker, Gilbert Norman. *The Naval Service of Canada: Its Official History*. *Vol. I, Origins and Early Years*. Ottawa: Kings Printer, 1962.

US Department of Energy Hanford. Handford Site. www.hanford.gov.

Index

141

Acknowledgements

Over the course of 20 years, I interviewed many veterans about the war on the West Coast. Almost all of them are gone now. We want to acknowledge their contributions—be it on the ground, in the air, at sea or on these pages.

About the Authors

Brendan Coyle was born and raised in New Westminster, BC. He is the author of the bestselling book *War on our Doorstep*. His freelance articles on BC historical topics have appeared in the *Times-Colonist, Vancouver Sun* and *Province* newspapers as well as in various diving publications. In 2003, Brendan addressed the American Battlefield Protection Program of the National Park Service in New York on the importance of preserving the Kiska Island battlefield in Alaska.

Melanie Arnis lives with her husband, Brendan Coyle, in Steveston, BC. Melanie has been an educational assistant supporting children with special needs for the last 30 years. She has written and edited articles and newsletters in many volunteer capacities, as well as collaborating with Brendan on *Enemy Offshore!* and editing his other writings.